WHERE EDGES DON'T HOLD

WHERE EDGES DON'T HOLD

A Small Island Miscellany

Christina Marsden Gillis

Copyright © 2017 Christina Marsden Gillis
All rights reserved.

ISBN-13: 9781540487643
ISBN-10: 1540487644
Library of Congress Control Number: 2016919588
CreateSpace Independent Publishing Platform
North Charleston, South Carolina

For John and Christopher, islanders both

Contents

Acknowledgments   ix

Preface: Unfinished Island   xiii

1 Geography in Motion   1

    Round and Round   5

    Edging   9

    Down Under   15

2 Recognition   25

    Miniatures   27

    Island Writing   31

    By Taxi   37

Changing Places   49

3   QUARRIES   55

Visiting the Stone   59

Good and Lawful Deeds   71

Departure   85

Desertion   99

On Duck   105

Diamonds   121

4   CROSSINGS   131

Crossing the Bar   135

Strings   139

Decorum   145

Bodies in Motion   149

Fencing   153

ABOUT THE AUTHOR   159

Acknowledgments

This book began with the idea of bringing together in one place a group of essays that I had published in various journals, with different audiences, but all dealing in some way with what it means to live on a small island. I envisioned readers who identified with the emerging field of Island Studies as well as those who were interested in the ways we experience and interpret place. Islands have particular appeal for all those who have visited them or even just viewed them as far-off bits of land on a distant horizon. "What is it like to live on an island?" I am frequently asked. This collection is my attempt to answer that question.

I am particularly indebted to the editors of *Island Journal*, published by the Island Institute in Rockland, Maine, where "Good and Lawful Deeds" "On Duck," and "Unfinished Island" have all appeared, enhanced by Peter Ralston's brilliant photographs. I had the good fortune as well to publish "On Duck" originally in *Raritan* and "Unfinished Island" in *Women's Studies*. My appreciation goes to Jackson Lears and

Wendy Martin respectively. "Diamonds" came out in *Hotel Amerika*; "Departure," in a slightly different form and with a different title ("Frost") was published in *Bellevue Literary Review*, whose nonfiction editor Jerome Lowenstein provided special encouragement to a non-medical professional writing about an island in Maine.

Parts of "Fencing," the final essay in the book, appeared originally in "Seeing Differently: Place, Art, and Consolation," published as a chapter in *Emotions, Identity, Mortality*, edited by Douglas Davies and Chang-Won Park (Ashgate, UK, 2012).

A collection of essays, however personal the point of view, always depends to some degree on what the writer has read. A number of works have informed my thinking in the pieces that appear here, most cited directly in the text but some sitting more unobtrusively in my imagination, their contributions not specifically identifiable.

Of writers and poets I address directly, the short list must include Gotts Island's own Ruth Moore, but also Elizabeth Bishop and Tove Jansson. On my much longer list of writers and scholars who have addressed the experience of place, whether islanded or not, the most important are Barbara Hurd, *Walking the Wrack Line*; Tim Robinson, *Stones of Aran: Pilgrimage*; Gary Lawless, in *Killock Stones* (ed. George Putz et al); William Least Heat Moon, *Blue Highways*; Andy Goldsworthy, *Enclosures*; JB Jackson, *Discovering the Vernacular Landscape*; Bonnie Costello, *Reinventing Landscape in Modern American Poetry*;

Patricia Hampl, *I Could Tell You Stories*, James Hamilton-Paterson, *Seven-Tenths: The Sea and Its Thresholds*; Kathleen Dean Moore, *Pine Island Paradox*; John Fowles, *Islands*; Tim Ingold, *The Perception of the Environment: Essays on Livelihood, Dwelling and Skill*; Perry Westbrook, *Biography of an Island*; Elizabeth Hallam and Jenny Hockey, *Death, Memory, and Material Culture*; Jeffrey Cohen, "Stories of Stone," Yi-Fu Tuan, *Escapism*; Eleanor Motley Richardson *Hurricane Island: The Town That Disappeared*; Charles McLane, *Islands of the Mid-Maine Coast*; Sanford Phippen, ed, *High Clouds Soaring, Storms Driving Low: The Letters of Ruth Moore*; Lynn Stegner and Russell Rowland, ed., *West of 98*; Peter Blanchard, *They Were An Island*; and Rita Kenway, *Gotts Island, Maine: Its People 1880-1992*.

To all of the above, and to all who have helped us understand the dynamic relationships between people and place, I am indebted. Nor should the work of visual artists be overlooked in this regard. My friend and inspiration Peter Ralston, for example, has helped me—and countless others—*see* place, particularly the islanded place, and I am deeply appreciative of having Peter's photograph of the Gotts Island bar on the cover of this book.

Last but certainly not least, my book, as a whole, owes much more to the active encouragement of John Gillis, with whom I have shared decades of summers on Gotts Island, and whose own extensive explorations of the meaning of islands and shores have launched many a conversation on the meaning of edges. Even more, the book would not be the same without John's drawings depicting the island we both know so well. They provide another response to the question of "what it is like to live on an island." To John, and to our son Christopher Gillis, fellow islander of the next generation, I dedicate this book.

Berkeley, CA
January 2017

Preface

UNFINISHED ISLAND

The ledges path leads from my back field in a southeasterly direction toward the sea. On a small island in Maine all paths lead ultimately to the sea. This one cuts through a spruce forest where deep mosses fill in the spaces between old trees that are falling away; it passes by clumps of new young trees thick and vigorous with early growth. But when it arrives at the ledges that rise up in the island's interior, it is interrupted by a rectangular cut in the granite. This is not a natural feature. It is a place where stone has been removed, and it marks what would have been called in local parlance a "motion."

We do not think of stone as endowed with agency. Place is supposed to stay put; the rock which once occupied this place on the ledges path could only have been purposefully moved by a human hand to serve some particular purpose. It may have become one of the rectangular granite blocks that form the foundation of our house; or perhaps it was transformed into our now worn and lopsided front door step. There is a story here, but it is almost 150 years old and has faded into the past. What is real is the space that remains, the place where the non-present seems eerily present: an invisible force.

But rock, we know, does move. "Motion" thus suggests to the imagination the slow movement, over millennia, of the bedrock of the island. As New England farmers know, the rock pushes up from below. It is a slow and relentless movement. Its pace and rhythm are far different from that of the nearby sea. Movement on the land is the object of archaeology and history; land-based knowledge is framed in linear time. But on the small island where I am a summer resident, where the sea is ever present, other stories present themselves, stories we experience less in linear trajectory than in the repeated motion of the tides.

On an island, place of edges, the ocean provides a counter-narrative, non-linear in what it reveals; "time's arrow" is modified by the rhythmic cycle of the sea as it encounters, and ever transforms, the shore. Historical, archaeological, or even narrative, knowledge is challenged by its meeting with the sea that offers up its own kind of knowing. We need to stretch, even confound, our usual frames to take account of such knowledge.

"Loss is the story about what happens next." The words are not mine. I borrow them from writer Barbara Hurd who used them as she walked the place where a receding tide had left a line left by bits of shells, pebbles and other fragments of detritus from the sea. A wrack line marks the tide that has gone out but tells us at the same time that ever changing, it will return.

Like Hurd I am interested in disappearance and return ("what comes next"), a process wherein loss remains not so much a static emptiness as a precursor of movement. A shore, an edge, is a place in motion. I know about loss, and having spent all the summers of my adult life as a summer resident on this small island in Maine, I know about edges. The goal is to emphasize not fixity and stasis but movement–a story, a narrative that goes on, ever changing, from past, to present, and beyond.

On a small island that is continually subject to the movement of the ocean, whose ostensible borders are constantly in motion, what always happens next is another tide. The rhythm and constant motion of the tide determine life on the island, in a sense part of life itself. Poet Elizabeth Bishop alluded to such movement in "North Haven," where, eulogizing fellow poet Robert Lowell–like Bishop a sometime summer island resident–she noted that with the death of her friend she can now only "pretend" that the island has "shifted since last summer," and is now "drifting . . . a little north, a little south." In the face of Lowell's death, North Haven Island may appear to be "afloat in mystic blue," but remains nonetheless "anchored in its rock." For Lowell, and for the island, there can be no more real change or "rearrangement." Motion, like poetry making, has stopped. The rocky edge of North Haven has become firm: a discreet edge.

But for the living, change, and motion, are still in play: we move along a path or old trail, we explore the place we know, we move in and out of time–historical and current–and we experience an edge that is not an end. For islands, and their paths, do not have "ends "in the usual sense: each supposed end is also a beginning, each edge determined by a constantly moving tide.

More than two decades since the sudden death of my younger son, I am drawn to what happens next. Though never entirely absent from consciousness, we come to feel loss in different ways. End points and borders are more porous than firm; fences prove impermanent. The white wood fence that had islanded the Gotts Island cemetery for decades rotted out in the summer of 2012. To all of us living on the island, it was unthinkable that the graves, some dating to the late eighteenth century, stand in unbounded ground; even if they are ultimately fictions, we need our boundaries. The old fence had to be replaced. Hence, with volunteer labor, a new one, somewhat changed in design, was put in place exactly where the old one had been. But just like the old fence, the replacement does not necessarily demarcate an end point. Photographer Peter Ralston, a valued friend of the island, got it right when he depicted in a stunning image of the cemetery not so much the fixity of death as its connection with life: in his photograph three young girls turn somersaults in the field in front of the cemetery fence. And as always, beyond the sharp focus of the photograph, lies the ocean, moving and shimmering in bright sunlight.

The ways we perceive, experience, create and remember place are infinite. With the line between land and sea ever fluctuating, old metaphors of isolation and insularity, whether of a small land mass or of self, are inadequate. The island concentrates, or even distills, experience, but it offers long vistas as well. We can locate images from memory in specific places, we can transpose a mental map onto a topographically defined location; but lived experience is never simply frozen or memorialized in a place that is itself moving and changing, both embraced by and embracing the sea. A small island, though apparently girded by its granite belt, is not necessarily contained, either in time or in space.

I know these things because I live them.

1

Geography in Motion

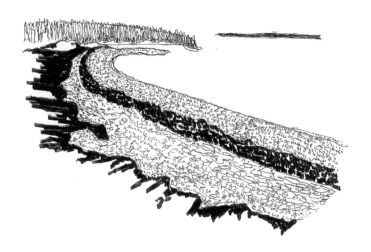

Here at a small field's ending pause
Where the chalk wall falls to the foam and its tall ledges
Oppose the pluck
And knock of the tide,
And the shingle scrambles after the suck-
-ing surf, and a gull lodges
A moment on its sheer side.

WH Auden, "On This Island"

In the rich sands of the ancient shell heap where the open field meets the shore, open to the sun, the daisies sink roots down into past generations and burst forth in profusion. The archaeologists tell us that the shell heap by the ocean's edge is about a thousand years old. Clam and mussel shells of how many meals past, remnants of shore creatures long dead, have been returned to the soils to nourish the daisies that rise white, saucy, and jubilant, above the tide line, above the clamor and pull of the surf.

Auden describes an island's edge where the ledges of a chalk wall "oppose" the movement of the sea. But the land is hardly static. The shingle "scrambles" with the pull of the tide. The gull rests ("lodges") for only a moment before moving on. The shore is a zone in motion, its processes of change never ending. On the island I know, the daisies will continue each year to compete for space in the white chalky soil until they too join the fertile layers of a thousand years duration.

The ocean moves round and round, the edges transform themselves in response to the tides, the rock moves silently and inexorably beneath our feet, and memory, in this place of continual motion, rests, like Auden's seagull, only momentarily before responding to, and joining once again, the "knock and pluck" of its ocean surround.

ROUND AND ROUND

> *On the day of our arrival [on the largest of the Aran islands] we met an old man who explained the basic geography: "the ocean," he told us, "goes around the island."*
>
> Tim Robinson,
> *Stones of Aran: Pilgrimage*

As recorded in his account of his first Aran Island experience, Tim Robinson took seriously what the old man said. He found that "the ocean encircles Aran like the rim of a magnifying glass, focusing attention to the point of obsession." And he went on to write what he calls the "pilgrimage" on which he and his wife embarked, a route that, following the coast of the eight-mile long island, would ultimately include detours, backtracks, and short cuts. But of course, in the old man's geography, it was not so much the path that we humans follow that was of interest; it was the ocean itself that "goes around the island." He turned things inside out, looked from the sea to the land. The ocean that "goes around" is endowed with movement and agency equal to, and sometimes overshadowing, that of the human rambler on the path,

But yet I am one of those ramblers, and the walk is central to my story. On a small island, one much smaller than the one Tim Robinson describes, I want to describe not so much a line connecting a series of destination points as an active encounter that has no clearly defined beginning or end. The walk bespeaks motion and movement. Like writing itself it seeks to open up new paths in the land it traverses. It may wander from one theme to another. Mine is a subjective geography, the place it describes deriving from–as well as making possible– individual reminiscence and connections, sometimes personal, sometimes with the visions and insights of observers and writers I do not know personally. Interactions with place trace a dynamic process. They help us "figure ourselves to ourselves" Robert Macfarlane has said. Place helps give form to thought. Animated in memory, so-called points of interest are neither, in themselves, stations in a pilgrimage nor identifiable spots on a putative route-map. Rather like the ocean itself, the journey simply "goes around."

With a sense of freedom I move over the surface of this island, through old spruce forests, over the massive granite, across the muddy low tide ooze. I traverse a familiar space, its interior and its edges, and know it again, over and over. Steps trigger memories, both serious and superficial: we remember the last time we walked this trail, rather slowly, with our old friends Lance and Marjorie, enjoying the day and happily unaware that Marjorie would be diagnosed two weeks later with terminal cancer and Lance would live his final years with Parkinson's. And there was the day when John, my husband, pushing the wheelbarrow of groceries out to the head and the little cottage we were renting that summer, hit a stump in the trail and the ten pounds of sugar I needed to make raspberry jam tumbled in a white pyramid into the rock and mosses. Forty years later, I still think of that sugar and wonder if the ground is sweeter in the spot of the spill.

I have written of this island before, how its landscape as well as its history—the loss of its original community and culture—offered, by reflection and refraction, consolation in the face of the loss of my son in a tragic accident. Just as important, because I am myself transient on this island, returning each summer from another, distant coast, the change and motion I experience here reinforce but also render more acceptable, the transitory nature of life itself.

The agency of place has long been central to my interests: what happens there? What does place make visible to us? How do place and memory connect, the one enabling the other? I am far from the first to engage these questions. The language of others who have taken similar journeys also informs my personal geography of the island. Writers like Tove Jansson, whom, alas, I must read in translation from the Swedish, but whose imaginative wit and intelligence strikes notes that are both familiar and enlightening. Maine island writer and poet Ruth Moore, whose house I literally inhabit, would have looked out through the same kitchen window as I to the broad vista of field, cemetery, and sea. Our friend Eric Hopkins, whose paintings of islands and sea have become iconic in Maine, once drew for us a sketch of that view, labeling it "Ruth's view." Her representations of what she saw and the voice in which she wrote, are far different from mine; but yet, the work of another island writer provides a valuable lens for my own view. It means that the process, the round and round journey that responds to the ever-moving sea, goes on.

EDGING

"All goes outward and onward"

Walt Whitman, *Song of Myself*

The galleries of the Stornaway historical museum, on the island of Lewis in the Scottish Hebrides, are crowded with school children on this dull chilly morning in June. They jostle and push, peer and point. "The grim reaper," a small boy quietly remarks as he signals the diorama of a dark hooded figure in what appears to be a murky cave or hut. His tone bespeaks the Calvinism that still so famously characterizes these Scottish islands and the barren, treeless landscape in which it is seemingly encoded. But the diorama is in fact an artist's notion of a sixth-century Christian monk, sitting in his cell on another barren Hebridean island. There were many such islands, many such ascetics, the text accompanying the exhibit informs us. An elaborate chart describes how the routes of St. Columba's sixth-century ministry, centered to the south, on the island of Iona, spread through the Scottish islands; we imagine the monks clinging to lives spent in the isolation of rocky cells and rough huts. What epiphany did these Christians seek at the margin? What need to live so close to an edge, to count time in the ever-changing tides?

An island, the most "edged" of spaces, would have meant to these holy men both containment and separation. It offered physical removal from a broader secular life and a location for spiritual contemplation: a "desert place in the sea," the monk Cormac is said to have called it. But whatever knowing of self in relation to God Cormac and his contemporaries may have sought, they found as dwelling place a zone of movement and transition. At the edge where two worlds come together–land and sea, even life and death–they could experience a special kind of knowing. I call it edge knowing.

"It would be enough," poet Wallace Stevens wrote in "The Ultimate Poem Is Abstract," "If we were ever, just once, at the middle, fixed/In This Beautiful World of Ours and not as now/ Helplessly at the edge." But do we really want to be standing or "fixed" in the middle? The speaker at the edge is "helpless" only to the degree that she neither controls nor possesses the object of her gaze. In Walt Whitman's terms, she is privileged, rather, to look both "outward and onward": she is positioned both spatially and temporally in a dynamic space.

The edge that presumably delineates place–the latter itself never a static entity–is a site of motion and change, both adjustments and erosions. My island is a place of edges, its pathways either following the contour of the edge or leading to an edge. I could say that the major path on Gotts Island, the "town road" that traverses the island, begins at one edge and ends at another; but this is the case only if I can identify which edge is the beginning and which the end. By the same token, where, exactly, is the edge? The neck, where the major body of the island is linked to the much smaller, bulbous portion that constitutes its furthest eastern point, grows more narrow each year. Boulders and fallen, rotting trees lie tangled together on a small stony beach beneath the high bank that is gradually eroding away. These same trees not so many years ago stood upright on the land above. This edge is literally moving; in time—though not my lifetime or that of my grandchildren– the eastern end of the island may become completely separate. The earth crumbles; the sea comes ever closer.

I move along a boundary that is not fixed, a site of impermanence. Shifting and uneven, the irregular tidal line is marked by the residue of seaweed fronds, odd and fragmented shells, small bits and pieces thrown up by the sea to mark a place in the wet sand, only then to disappear again in the next high tide. Subtraction and absence are never permanent here: disappearance will give way to appearance, absence to fulfillment. Do I become more flexible, more available to the power of change and transition, as I walk this edge? Or, do I become dependent on change and the faith that the apparent erasure will be itself erased?

Perhaps I need the fulfillment that follows the absence; I need to know that the creatures and weed that populate the seemingly empty expanse of mud, the scampering crabs, the clam that spouts under my foot at low tide, will disappear to my eye but still be there, under the surface. I will see water where six hours ago I saw a muddy, stony shore. A boat that sat ungainly and grounded on the tidal mud will now float gracefully free.

With no static border, there is no fixed point where things–field, place, or person–come to an abrupt end or simply "runs out." Continued movement cancels such endings; changes, losses and accumulations enable an imaginative grappling with temporality and flux. For Prince Edward Island writer Shauna McCabe, the shore presents itself as a "palimpsest, bearing the imprint and erasures of earlier processes and contemporary ones, remnants and modern forms."

Some of those remnants, we discovered this summer, lie deep in the tidal mud, to be revealed only by accident. After a large barge carrying building materials had arrived at the island at high tide and gouged out deep hollows in the pebbly beach, we saw for the first time, at low water, a scattering of rocks and shards of rotted wooden piers. Here were the scant material remains of the fish shacks I had seen in old island photographs. Revealed for several hours, then, with a rising tide, covered once more, they constitute a history that belongs to the cyclical rhythm of the shore.

Given such flux, neither the edge nor a supposed middle can be precisely identified. And there is no need to do so. For the island's edges neither confine nor contain. They belong rather to what Herman Melville called–in referring, in *Moby Dick*, to the island of Queequeg's origin– a "true place," the place that cannot be known or described merely in terms of spatial points on a map.

I think that when Ruth Moore, the island writer in whose family home I now live, said in a letter to a friend that she did not want to "lie about place," she meant that she wanted her island–the island she experienced in her childhood as well as the one she created in fiction and poetry–to remain a "true place": named of course, even identifiable on a map, but nonetheless retaining the mystery that derives from being known only partially. Something always remains, "out there," beyond the so-called edge. To speak with a littoral voice –with "tongues of granite, tongues of salt," as poet Gary Lawless described Moore's work–is to know that the history, lore, and topographic details do not tell the whole story. Granite and salt, rock and ocean are, more importantly, signifiers of the ever-moving boundary between land and sea, past and present, the seen and unseen. This is a place where the poet can look beyond an edge, envisioning evanescent forms that "loom" like phantom islands in distant waters: mutability wrought in this case by particular atmospheric conditions.

In a poem titled "Time to Go," the poet and her interlocutor, the sole remaining inhabitant of the island, transform the island from a chamber of the absent to an open-ended lens through which they view time and change that are always present, whether encoded in memory and imagination, or even, geologically, in the rocky substrate. The island artist, the artist of the edge, sees–and creates– in the broad scope of sea and sky a kind of third space that eludes classification and takes precedence over the polar realities of "sea" and "land," the real and the imagined, past and present time.

Our frames must be tenuous, places where memory, uncontained, can live. I witnessed only once, and from a moving boat rather than the shore of the island, the "looming" that Ruth Moore knew and described. But I remember well the sudden appearance and disappearance of that phenomenon, the surprise and even amazement that it occasioned. I hope I may one day see that vision again, but since this is an unusual sight in the summer months when I am in Maine, I cannot really expect it.

And so I seek my visions at the island's edge, where perpetual tidal shift and movement reflect and refract the ongoing work of memory. Here I have learned that a loss sustained years ago is also mutable: apprehended, felt, and seen differently over time. The island offers neither an antidote to loss nor a timeless space where memory is fixed and permanent. I do not know exactly where memory, and the stories it enables, will go.

From my son's gravesite in the Gotts Island cemetery I can look down into the pool below, now full with the high tidal waters, now empty with the patterns of grasses, rocks, pebbles and tidal mud all strangely visible. These are the quiet times. But about two hours before the tide's highest or lowest point, the waters, in feverish motion, will surge with power far greater than that of mere mortal observers.

DOWN UNDER

Northwood's field, just adjacent to our own, had always looked to me smooth and rock-free. But I hadn't noticed the rocks that are *in* the ground, their traces just barely visible on the surface. Northwood's eye is sharper than mine. He saw the stone, and he wanted it removed.

That's why Scott Swann and his backhoe are creating such a terrible roaring noise today. Contrary to what one might think, island living can be very noisy. It's not only the machinery that individual families own—the chain saws, lawn mowers, log splitters, all-track vehicles, and generators. It's also as if the bedrock of the island, like a great sounding board, echoes back and amplifies all the sounds we humans make. From my front deck I can hear footsteps on the crunchy stones of the bar a good quarter of a mile away.

With deft management of the backhoe, Scott is tearing out the rocks in the field. They may try to hide but they will not escape. Even a small bit of visible rock gets in the way of his lawn mower, Northwood says. And he's had experience with this problem: as custodian of the island cemetery, he'd had to remove the field rocks that had been placed in the cemetery decades ago to mark the burial of the unknown Italian quarrymen from Black Island who drowned when their barge went down. The rocks had made grass cutting simply too challenging. They had to go. And no one now knows just where in the cemetery the bodies of those quarrymen are.

It's people against rocks, an old and familiar story. Generations of New England farmers, including those with small-scale plots on Maine islands, must have viewed themselves, like Northwood, in perpetual conflict with rocks. So they gathered them up and built the famed walls. Engineers would call the walls examples of "heap structures," held together by forces of gravity and friction, but I am drawn more to the description by William Least Heat Moon, who explains, in *Blue Highways*, that in building a stone wall, he could sense "an urging in the rocks, a behest to be put in just so, to be set where they would hold against the shifts of the earth, against the twists of the roots. . . . The rocks were moving us [and] we just followed the will of the wall."

As he operated the backhoe in Northwood's field, I doubt that Scott experienced the "urging" or the "will" of the rock. But British sculptor Andy Goldsworthy apparently did, explaining in a journal entry his sense of guilt in excavating, "uprooting," field stones in Scotland for the "Sheepfolds Project," inspired by the actual stone enclosures built by Scottish (and English) sheep farmers. Goldsworthy's excavating machine "claws" at the rock. The artist tells us in his book titled *Enclosure* that he was particularly disconcerted when one dislodged stone, "almost too heavy to be moved," began by its own agency to roll, threatening the power of both man and machine. "It seems," he observed, "as though the stones have been brought to life as they have been pulled out of the ground. All stones make a journey, whether it is through the processes of fire, sedimentation, compression or upheaval, and these boulders particularly so in that they have been deposited by glacial action. Movement is part of their character."

The geological explanation of movement—volcanic activity, sedimentation, compression, and upheaval—translates in Goldsworthy's account to a kind of "life" and "character" that can be felt epochs later by the human hand. It is the "urging in the rock" that William Least Heat Moon described. And it is akin to the spiritual force that Mircea Eliade describes in cultures where rock is considered sacred. In *Patterns of Comparative Religion*, Eliade tells us that in megalithic burial practice, for example, stone was the means of protecting life against death: "Imprisoned in a stone, the soul [of the dead] could be forced only to act beneficently." At the opposite end of the life-death trajectory, Eliade cites belief in the so-called "fertilizing" power of stone found in some South Asian, as well as European, cultures, in some instances giving rise to rituals that persisted, despite ecclesiastical pressure to the contrary, into the later nineteenth century. Stone, Eliade has written, always drew its religious significance from extra-human powers believed to emanate from God; or even more directly, from a belief that God Himself is present in the stone.

Eleventh and twelfth century texts called lapidaries also endowed rocks with special capacities to affect the world.

Medievalist Jeffrey Cohen has described how rocks in these texts are "embedded within networks of agency. . . simultaneously constrained and enabled by other actors [such as] rivers, angels, animals, intensities of heat and light." The whole meshwork, Cohen points out, "pulses with movement."

I don't know if Gotts Island's poet, Ruth Moore, was aware of any of these accounts, but I do know that she also saw power and force in stone. In a poem titled "Rocks" she juxtaposes science and the supernatural, and like sculptor Andy Goldsworthy, moves from a geological explanation of movement in rock into a meditation that sharply challenges any notion of the inert materiality of stone: "The rocks of the earth hold secrets," she writes, and what lies within the stone defies scientific explanation: the "lapidary" can cut the stone thin, examine its inner layers, and determine a "mathematical design" that traces a geological history. But sometimes, the poet says, "a difference creeps in" unexplained by "scientific logic"; it is, she says, "some hidden consciousness," whose secret will never be clear to us. In their capacity to "tell us how old is old," the rocks utter both history and geological truth. They are the island's first "historians," never "inexpressive, unyielding, [or] immobile."

"Rocks" calls up the enormity of stone, the vast ledges that ring the shore of the island Ruth Moore knew so well. But living on Gotts, Moore would have experienced rock in many guises and forms. She would have known as well the oblong block of granite that still serves as the front door step at her family home; and she would have remembered the large chunks of stone on which the house rests. People on Maine islands live with, as well as on, stone. And the stone they live with, those doorsteps or foundation blocks, all deriving from local, very small-scale, sites, connect them directly to the long history traced in the island's bedrock. Stone, even if ripped free from its original place and incorporated into human histories, brings with it a record of movement in time.

On a small island, the original place, the site of origin, may not be hard to find. Walking the ledges path that runs from my back field in a southeasterly direction toward the sea, I come to a rectangular cutout space in the granite outcropping. There is a peculiar vacancy in this sharply delineated space; it's as if the margins trace the outline of the missing piece in a puzzle. I'm looking at presence and nonpresence all at the same time. The stone that became the doorstep or the foundation block, perhaps bringing with it its "secrets" and "hidden consciousness," would literally have been moved from this spot, human agency requisite to the task. But in the quiet and apparent fixity of this space, a history, another kind of movement in time, another agency, asserts itself.

Like stone, language also has secrets, holds out mysteries. Did Ruth Moore know, for example, that this empty place in the granite, this remainder of a quarrying spot, would, in local language, have been called a "motion"? Here is a word–it appears in accounts of quarrying not only in

Maine but also in Missouri and South Dakota–that resonates with the suggestion of inexplicable agency; but its derivation remains unclear. It may refer solely to human activity, as in "process of moving," "change of place," or "act of moving the body": a man would literally have moved small blocks of stone that he was chiseling out. Or, when one plot was exhausted, he would have moved to another site. But this is only conjecture. In the quarries of South Dakota–we're speaking here of the late nineteenth and early twentieth centuries– a motion referred simply to a "cutting area." In a quarrying region in St. George, on the Penobscot Bay of Maine, it meant, specifically, a "one man operation" in which no mechanical apparatus was used.

None of these explanations supports Ruth Moore's comment on the "invisible secrets" in the stone, or the accounts in William Least Heat Moon and Andy Goldsworthy that endow stone itself with its own agency. In only one example in the OED list of definitions does the word "motion" (singular) refer to the thing that is moved: this is a sixteenth-century usage, and the object moved is not stone but a puppet, the latter given agency by the puppeteer, or "motion man."

But still we can look to movement and motion in terms of time and history: rock as time's calendar, the poet's "historian." History, even shrunk to the scale of human time, goes on. The front door step, having seen so many decades of feet passing over it, so many frosts and thaws, driving spring rains and hot summer sun, has become worn and lop-sided. In the human community, as described–and decried–in Moore's poem, a grand narrative is reduced to a drive to stake out property boundaries. Time and history give way to space and ownership:

> Beginning at a large rock with a hole in it at the end of a stonewall, said point of beginning being the southwest corner bound of a certain lot of land described in deed from Ruth Moore to the grantors herein dated April 25, 1958 . . .[thence proceeding] along a stone wall . . . to a stake driven in the ground.

So reads the deed to my own island property. I know that rock with the hole. Just last summer, stumbling with a surveyor through the juniper and brambles, I found it just where the 1958 deed directed. The rock is distinctive; it does its job well. But why the hole, and how did it get there? The writing on the original 1812 deed to the property is no longer decipherable. If the secret lies there, it remains intact.

As for Northwood's rocks, they had no doubt been buried a long time in his field. They were there, as Moore recounts, when the "first summer people," the Native Americans, came out to the island five thousand years ago; when the first members of the founding Gotts family arrived at the end of the eighteenth century; and when William Harding, burned out of his original place on Duck

Island in 1883, came out to Gotts and acquired, around 1890, the property that Northwood now owns.

Animals grazing in summer, children riding sleds down the hill and over the snow-covered field, wagons bringing supplies up from the shore–all would have moved over the small outcroppings that hid a much larger force. So much life was lived above and around those rocks. The rocks may have been markers, perhaps home plate for a local baseball team, perhaps the goal in countless games of hide and seek. Or, a rock may have served as anchor for the farm shed or outbuilding whose imprint had been clearly legible in the damp grasses of the field. When the backhoe finishes its work, the pattern in the earth will become invisible, the trace of the past a mere scar in the newly turned up soil.

For the backhoe has not yet finished. It is still searching out the rock, clutching its prey, and lumbering off again and again with loud grunting sounds, a huge boulder held aloft in its jaws. Again and again I hear the roar of the returning monster, coming back for another load. And another. All the long afternoon, the groans of the engine continue, clawing, clawing, at the soil in its frenzy to pry up the rocks.

We make wry jokes. "Maybe with the rocks in his field gone, Northwood's house will shift to the south," we say. And we imagine: the earth knows that it has lost something; nature will fight for its own, justifying itself against those who devote themselves to its control. Remove the rock and the world tilts out of balance.

Nor does the story end there. The pressure of frost and thaw will continue to push up rocks from below. The movement must be unceasing, an immeasurable amount of rock lying beneath the surface of the island. I think about how deep it goes. I imagine our own house sitting on a gigantic plate of granite, the small outcropping by the lilac bush near our kitchen window the mere vestige of a great totality. It's the unseen, the unknown, that intrigues me, the life beneath the surface. This is the rock that connects our field to the great slabs of granite that mark the coast of the island and, much further beyond, to the hills and crags of Acadia National Park across the Bay on the mainland. The granite is a giant anchor, ballast in this coastal world.

But I doubt that Northwood thought about any of this. By the end of the afternoon he was more than satisfied with Scott's work. There was only one problem. He directed my attention the next day to two small stakes in the ground. They marked the presence of two more rocks that had escaped the backhoe the day before and now dared to peep up from the depths.

"We'll get them when Scott comes back next week," he said.

2

Recognition

"Heavens, I recognize the place, I know it!"

"Poem," Elizabeth Bishop

I imagine Elizabeth Bishop gazing at the miniature painting in her hand; I imagine her pleasure in the recognition that she "knows" the place. And in her exclamation of discovery, I read joy, even exultation.

This is the pleasure of knowing again. And with that knowing comes the recall that in Bishop's poem, and in our lives, re-animates the experiences of a particular place and the web of relationships that are part of mutual knowing. In this case, a representation in art, in visual form, sparks the recognition; the miniature captures the experience. The recognizable place can be re-known, re-called, taking on meaning that exceeds the specific content represented in the artist's image.

In its Latin root, recognition bespeaks knowing as an active process. It means knowing again in a different temporal frame. Such recalling is a reminder that nothing stands still. Bishop's poem, titled "Poem," is thus profound in its meditation on what we see, what we remember, and just as important, what we can know again. The image recalls a place to mind, but never in the same way. It opens up layers of meaning embedded in time; it reanimates the remembered past.

We look, we recognize, and we know again. But like the tides that are ever in motion, the experience is never the same.

MINIATURES

I recognized the place I saw in the 1920's painting of Gotts Island. The artist, one Harold B. Warren, had created it from the perspective of someone just emerging from the woods, heading west, into the village, on the town road. My house is on the left, the Archibalds' on the right. The Kenways' roof is just visible below the brow of the hill.

The painting, as I can see in the catalogue image, is larger than the miniature that Elizabeth Bishop described in "Poem" ("the size of an old-style dollar bill"), but still small (12"x12"). The tones of purplish light suggest late afternoon on a hazy day. The houses, not sharply defined, almost ghost-like, are shabby: "Look, there's that old addition that we removed when we renovated the house in 1990," we say. The town road runs much closer to the Archibalds' porch than it does now. That's because the current owner's grandmother planted the bridal wreath bushes to keep the road –really a track or wide path– from working its way any closer to her house.

I'm looking into the past, the "way it was." First comes the pleasure of recognition, then, the realization that the painting as a piece of art, imbued with its purplish hues, is itself so pleasing (we will wish it belonged to us and not to the person mentioned in the gallery catalogue). Time de-familiarizes the scene–it doesn't look quite like that any more–but we easily know our own house, even with that strange lop-sided addition that always leaked at the place where it met the main structure, even with the space between our house and the town road wider than it now is: with the growth of the bridal wreath bushes, the road pushed away from the neighbor's house and closer to us. Features change, they move; but we still know them.

In "Poem," Elizabeth Bishop looks at a miniature of a familiar place and says, "I recognize the place, I know it." Like Bishop, we know what Mr. Warren's scene "must be." Bishop's poem is about knowing and what can be known in the miniature that she is looking at: knowing whose house is depicted, which church steeple occupies the middle distance, to whom those geese and cows must have belonged. "It's still loved," Bishop says. But just what is still loved? The place or the memory of the place called up in the picture? The two have "turned into each other." So attend to the detail, the poet tells us, to the memory and the life "compressed" on the artist's board. We are all subject to time: our "abidance" here is small. The flowers, the cows, the pooled water–all, like the "yet-to-be-dismantled" elms–will change. This too is a knowing.

Harold B. Warren created the small painting of Gotts Island years before I was born. I can only superimpose upon the scene the details of the physical place as I know it, recognizing the present in this small lens upon the past. Unlike Bishop, I cannot–have no need to–attest to the "reality" of a scene that is doubly distanced: first by the painter and then by time. When Bishop exclaims, "I recognize the place, I know it!" she means that she "knows" it because she knew it in the past. The miniature triggers connections with other family members, even with an Uncle George whom she never really knew but who, like herself, "knew this place." That knowing linked the two, and as the poet now addresses a younger family member ("he'd be your great-uncle"), the knowing, and the connection, stretches out to yet another generation. Place in the miniature, and in Bishop's poem, is animated through shared memory.

I turn the page in the catalogue where the Gotts Island painting appears and find a photograph of three gentlemen sitting on the porch of the Nowandthen cottage, built on the eastern, open-ocean shore of Gotts Island in 1904. This trio, according to the present owners of the Nowandthen, were connected with Little Cranberry Island (Islesford) and were known locally as the "Three Islesford Painters." Warren, painter of the Gotts Island scene, is on the far right in the photograph. The year is 1927. The men are dressed in white shirts, ties, straw hats, jodhpurs and what appear to be high boots that must have been intended for walking the mile-long trail out to the Nowandthen. They are the guests of the Burnham family, owners of the house. Inside, a servant may be preparing chowder for lunch (a Burnham family diary refers to the chowder making at the Nowandthen cottage). Or, maybe it's late afternoon. The men have completed their painting for the day, and the servant within is preparing not lunch but dinner. At any rate, the three are now relaxing, immersed in genteel conversation.

No doubt they are enjoying the view before them. I recognize, know well, the house and its porch where the three artists sit. It's all still there, remarkably little changed. I know the scene the men would have been looking at. Do they speak of the enormity of the granite that stretches out before them, the rock that bravely bears, impervious, the crashing of the surf? Do they discuss how they might catch on canvas the repeated and endless movement of water on stone? Or, does Mr. Warren speak, rather, of the place he has just, or will soon, paint: the place where the town road just enters the village, a place of stillness where the sky is rose purple, the field grasses blow gold, and the houses stand silent, tired and patient matrons watching for their men to return from the sea.

ISLAND WRITING

It takes an island writer to see islands in motion. Finnish writer Tove Jansson was such a writer. In "The Iceberg," a piece in her anthology titled, in English, *A Winter Book*, an unnamed child narrator–Jansson often portrayed her world through the eyes of children–rows out from her family's island home, sees a floating iceberg and seeks to claim it as her own. It "was waiting for me," the child says, " shining . . . beautifully but very faintly."

It's spring in the land. The iceberg is a contrast, all the more unreal. And it is unreachable; though the child wants to leap across the black water to grasp the floating ice that she sees as "trying to come to me," the two cannot meet. The floating matter in the "stern and forbidding" sea remains attainable only to the eye. When the child casts her flashlight on it, it becomes "an illuminated aquarium at night"–and then sails out to sea, shining " like a green beacon." The iceberg has life only so long as the flashlight plays upon it. Everything depends on the flashlight, whose batteries would last until sunrise, Jansson writes, because "they were always new when one had just moved to the country."

The iceberg incident typifies Tove Jansson's craft: the deftness of contrast, of juxtapositions: beginnings and endings, desire and frustration, the seduction of the unattainable visual phenomenon–and finally, the sudden return to ordinary reality with the statement that because it is still early summer, the batteries are new and will last a while. Playing with a flashlight in the dark is a child's delight that I have witnessed many times with my own grandchildren. And everyone who spends a summer on a small island with no electricity knows about flashlights and the crucial importance of batteries. On an island with no roads, a homely flashlight lights our way home on a narrow, pitch dark path; for Jansson's child narrator, a flashlight illumines a magic floating island of ice whose very existence depends upon the beam of light.

The Finnish archipelago and a small island in Maine are geographically distant sites. But I include Jansson in my small island meditation because she is, to me, a quintessential island writer. In her unique voice, she describes a journey I want to share, a journey through a world in motion.

Born and raised in Helsinki as the member of the Swedish-speaking minority in Finland, Jansson spent summers in her family's island country home, and much later, as an adult, lived with her partner on the farthest out island in the archipelago. *Summer Book*, Jansson's memoir cum fiction, provides another striking example of the island writer's perception of movement and the changing scale of things that a small island makes visible.

The ice island could not be fixed in place; it simply floated away. Like Jansson's child protagonist, I too must be willing to give up fixity. When I first began to write about islands, specifically the island in Maine where I have spent nearly fifty summers, I was drawn to a notion of permanence and to the ways that I could find a foothold in a particular place. I needed the notion of the island as bounded and secure: the house I can return to each summer, the fenced cemetery, doubly "islanded." I was writing then in response to catastrophic personal loss, and I needed a place to fix my grief, a place that would allow me to focus on the known, in both space and time. Only then could I contemplate the puzzle of inexplicable loss that remains ever unknown. To cope with my son's bizarre death, with that ultimate absence, I needed to know that his grave was in that fenced cemetery and would in a sense remain; I needed it where I could look out my kitchen window and see it: a fixed presence.

The island provided for me then, and still does, what Patricia Hampl called a "habitation" for thought and feeling. Knowing an island, I later came to see however, means recognizing also the movement and motion that Jansson represents in her short fictional pieces. I am in motion; the island is in motion. Like Jansson's child, I can cast my flashlight on it, but I can never claim it as my own.

James Hamilton-Paterson has argued that the notion of possession is inseparable from an attraction to small islands. Within a sea that can be seen as limitless, Hamilton-Paterson writes, the mere sight of an island "mobilizes the beginnings of possessiveness. . . .The unit of land which fits within the retina of the approaching eye is a token of desire."

I know the pleasure of the "approaching eye." I experience it each summer when we make our first trip out to the island, as well as each time we return to the island from an excursion "off." But mine is the eye of the summer nomad, who, in each return to the island, experiences movement toward a place of difference: a place in which she can both be at home and participate imaginatively in the creation of a landscape. Legally, my husband and I own a given property of about eleven acres. We have the deed to prove it. But contrary to Hamilton-Paterson's assertion, we know we do not own, legally or otherwise, the small island. We cannot possess an island in motion. Its granite borders are more porous than they appear. Like Jansson's iceberg, this island is not fixed.

I think of another of Tove Jansson's fictionalized children, another in one of those small jewel-like stories that portray, as I have suggested, a moving world. Consider "the Boat and Me." Here, a child wants to "encircle," in her boat, the whole Pellinge [Finland] archipelago, "uninhabited rocks and all, both the inner and outer parts."

The child sets off, and headed before the wind toward the "outermost promontory," suddenly sees "that the sea really needs a boat on it to be in control–I mean to be greater than everything else. Maybe it needs islands too, so long as they're small ones." As the boat rounds the rough promontory and comes into the lee, the child enters another environment: in the sheltered shallows a forest grows "down to the rocks on the shore, with the small islands sailing around like floating bouquets and everything's completely green."

Where is the edge in the child's point of view? What remains, what moves? The child herself is moving in the boat of course. She goes from the rough promontory to the quiet lee of the shore. But though the forests presumably maintain their place on that shore, the child sees everything as "completely green." The land has taken over the sea in this spot, and the apparently stable small islands are "sailing around like floating bouquets." So where is the fixed eye? The only fixity is that the child apparently knows whereof she speaks (and sees): she tells us she has been "here before."

The child is neither at the middle nor at the edge. She is everywhere and nowhere. She sees the trees of the forest as joined, in the color green, with the sea; she sees islands in motion. And she possesses nothing, understanding, rather, that it is the sea that likes to be in control, "needing" the small islands with which to define itself as the greater force.

Here again is Tove Jansson as island artist. And though she may have agreed with the writer/poet of my own island, Ruth Moore, that the island is a "microcosm of anywhere else," she, like Moore, demonstrates that the artist who writes of the most apparently bounded physical space is one whose perception is the least "insular," transcending borders in both time and space.

As an island writer, I want not to possess, but to suggest the ways that we can know an island. In an apparently illogical phrase, the mother of Jansson's boat child tells her to take along no inessential objects, departures being "never what you expect." It's an odd formulation. We would expect, rather, that it is the destination that remains occluded to our eye. But where we come out depends on what we take, or do not take, with us. What is essential, what is not? What lens shall we use? Where shall we go and whom will we speak with? The scenes that await us, the whole scopic experience of the island, will always be, at least in part, of our own making, participant in a larger, totalizing experience.

As the boat slows and we come round into the Gotts Island pool, the island's western shore, the half-dozen or so houses that cluster near the pool or at its edge, the sprinkling of moored boats, the hill along which several more houses arrange themselves, the rectangle of white cemetery fence–all are taken in by the "retina of my eye." Yes, it's all here, my eye tells me; the camera shot is adequate.

But only for that nanosecond. The boat is still moving; I am moving. I thought I knew the departure point but such knowledge, as the boat child's mother suggests, will depend ultimately on the destination. Best travel light and be ready to keep moving.

BY TAXI

I learned today that the modern Greek term *metaphori* means taxi. I could travel about in modern Athens in a metaphori. "I'm taking a metaphori," I could say. "I'm using a *metaphori* to get where I want to go."

Metaphor is a vehicle that gets us somewhere, motion integral to its function and meaning. Metaphor is about making connections, about movement from one place to the other. Metaphors drawn literally from the experience of moving through a physical environment may lend themselves to a heightened awareness of what Robert Macfarlane calls one's "interior terrain." But whatever the object of understanding, metaphor not merely adorns thought; it produces it as well. Words relating to knowledge production– theory, method, symbol, method–all derive from Greek roots connoting motion. Writer Rebecca Solnit has called metaphor the "transportation system of the mind."

Though one's knowledge of place, even a small island, is always far from complete or comprehensive, the use of some form of taxi is always useful to the endeavor. Without the metaphor, and without a connecting pathway, a narrator divorces herself from the surrounding environment. Place, whether islanded or not, is diminished in such a case, the knowledge it may yield truncated. I think of a writer, a confirmed urban dweller, whose "search for self" took her to a small island off the coast of New England; but once on the island, with which she was ostensibly familiar, her quest never extended very far from her own house. Close to the end of her narrative, when she finally makes a move to explore her island further, she discovers to her surprise that, hitherto unknown to her, other people are living there and have been for years.

This particular story of choosing a small island as the locus for sorting out one's life has little to do with knowing place. The so-called "interior terrain" is isolated from the external. Taking a taxi, whether literally or figuratively, would have seemed both unnecessary and impossible. The writer could of course have ventured out on foot; in so doing she may have come to know the island where she was living, and she may have discovered the value and pleasure of finding new metaphors. But without a bridge connecting her to the physical world, her island, as site for self-discovery and recovery, can only function as what writer Harrison-Patterson calls the "perfect territorial expression of the ego."

This account, one of myriads one could cite–from Defoe's Robinson Crusoe, to DH Lawrence's "Man Who Loved Islands," to contemporary writer Jonathan Franzen's narrative of his journey to Selkirk Island–actually draws on one particularly strong and resilient metaphor: the island as figure for isolation, separation, and boundedness. Only recently have scholars like John Gillis, Godfrey Baldacchino, and Ove Ronstrom, all practitioners in the growing field of Island Studies, begun to question the dominance of this idea. Looking at the various etymologies of words for "island" in North and Northwest European languages, for example, Ronstrom finds a complexity of meanings describing land *by water* but not necessarily *separated by water*. John Gillis finds that notions of separation and isolation became dominant only when islands ceased to hold a central place in human culture and economies, leaving continents to achieve dominance.

We can only wonder how much literature over the past 300 years would not have been written if the "island/isolation" pairing had had a much shorter life. To the contrary, it lives on strongly, still informing, for better or worse, and in various registers, our thinking about islands–and still blinding us to what other taxis might be available.

Visitors

Some writers play with metaphors, reveal limitations even as they create new ones of their own. In an April, 2011, *New Yorker* essay, Jonathan Franzen casts himself as an island sojourner in need of "being farther away." His journey takes him to remote Selkirk Island, the furthest westward island in the Chilean Juan Fernandez chain. The island, he says, "is not inviting." Like Duck Island off the southeast shore of Mount Desert Island in Maine, Selkirk is a breeding site for petrels (Franzen does not mention that the now uninhabited

Selkirk was once the site of a penal colony that housed up to 140 inmates). The writer is interested in birds; but, in part motivated by the death of his friend and fellow writer David Foster Wallace, he is also engaged in the classic search for personal recovery that he hopes to achieve through subjecting himself to isolation and difficulty. Importantly however, Franzen is not unaware of the irony inherent in his endeavor. Having achieved a steep and arduous climb to the island's high remote ridge and then spying a ranger's hut, he admits that he is drawn to the idea of spending the night there, as opposed to camping out; but, he says, the hut "made my already somewhat artificial project of solitary self-sufficiency seem even more artificial, and I resolved to pretend that it didn't exist." Similarly, in searching out the rare bird species said to inhabit the island, he observes, "When I go looking for a new bird species, I'm searching for a mostly lost authenticity, for the remnants of a world now largely overrun by human beings but still beautifully indifferent to us." Franzen has a mission. But he never does find the bird. The weather goes from bad to worse and even his faithful GPS proves of little help. Blinding rain, sharp cliffs, and rocks block his path; he becomes "afraid to take another step."

In a sense Franzen explores Selkirk Island by way of a firmly established and well-known taxi: the metaphor of the island as the protecting zone of the self, limited and defined. But this is ultimately too simple a vehicle for a skillful writer so acutely aware of where he is really going. Focusing on the obvious example of Defoe's Robinson Crusoe—for whom, the real-world eighteenth-century castaway

Alexander Selkirk is said to be the model—Franzen is drawn to critic Ian Watt's classis thesis that an emphasis on the individual was essential to the birth and development of the novel: how, in Crusoe, the "self had become an island." But fast-forward almost three centuries and Franzen finds the "individual. . . run amok . . . [and]the island . . . becoming the world." This was the twenty-first century world that Franzen's close friend, David Foster Wallace, could not tolerate: "Fiction was [Foster Wallace's] way off the island" he says, [and] when he couldn't write, he could only die." In a perhaps final irony, Franzen scatters on Selkirk— so-called founding site of the literature of the individual—some of the ashes of his fellow writer. Then, asserting that he is now content with the "incomplete," with not having sighted the bird he had hoped to see, he says that he "felt done with anger, merely bereft, and done with islands, too."

If Franzen is "done with islands," it means he is done with a certain kind of island thinking. He is done, we might say, with old metaphors of self that still powerfully hold sway in the Western imagination: the island as stand-in for individuation, retreat, and the often-attendant therapeutic notions of rehabilitation and recovery.

In island commentary, metaphors of separation and isolation have been far more pervasive than those of connection. But sometimes the latter do appear, albeit in odd ways. At a conference I attended on dementia and aging a linguist studying aphasia remarked that the apparently incoherent utterances of the aphasiac were actually "misshapen islands of a former self." In this case, the island is posited as a fragment of what was once whole. The metaphor acknowledges an earlier time, a "shape" that was once right but has come out of kilter. The "islanded" utterance of the aphasiac now sits alone in an empty sea upon whose surface small landmasses float like punctuation marks removed from the sentence or paragraph.

But even as the island as a figure of linguistic incoherence bespeaks the familiar trope of disconnection and isolation, it harks back to a whole that, though now lost, belonged to a defined moment in the past to which all later developments and changes refer. So too, geologically speaking, with islands: in a far different context, environmental philosopher Kathleen Dean Moore reminds us in *Pine Island Paradox* that though an island may be the symbol of isolation and exile, "any geographer will tell you that an island is in fact only a high point in the continuous skin of the planet . . . . It's a sign of the wholeness of being." Novelist John Fowles posits another kind of wholeness when he explains that he sees narrative structure as built of "islands" (key events of passages) within the "sea of story." He needs, he says, the "capacity to enisle"; but when complete, the whole narrative is likened to a connected "archipelago."

Which Taxi to Take?

We must decide then which taxi to take—or whether to take a taxi at all. Swedish ethnologist Ove Ronstrum worries about island metaphors and how they can get in the way of ethnological research in what he wants to call "real" islands. He fears that representation cast in metaphorical terms trumps "reality." The iteration of the island as generalized metaphor is highly suspect for a researcher and writer in a country that has well over 200,000 islands. A move among folk life researchers to cast the islanded place as "bounded and remote, archaic and endemic," renders islandness and insularity constitutive of what Ronstrum calls a "mythical geography" that blocks more serious analysis of island cultures.

Some taxis, then, may take us to the wrong place or simply bring us back to our starting point with no new understanding achieved; in others, we may pass through a given landscape too quickly to take full note of what we are seeing. ("I often see flowers from a passing car/That are gone before I can tell what they are," Robert Frost wrote in a poem appropriately titled "A Passing Glimpse"). Anthropologist Tim Ingold is also suspicious of speed and determined destination: while movement is the essential core of understanding in Ingold's view, the idea of destination, the route as simple connector between two loci, is not the way to go. The real point for Ingold is the traveler's involvement in the environment, her "practical engagements" with her surroundings.

A given place—and let me be more specific and speak of an islanded place—"owes its character" then to the experiences it affords to those who spend time in it. We know place through moving through and interacting with it: through dwelling in it.

Dwellers

For the first twenty summers or so that we spent at our Gotts Island home, it was impossible to look westward to neighboring Placentia Island and not think about Art and Nan Kellam, the couple who lived alone, year-round, in that remote place. Now both dead (Art in 1985, Nan in 2002), their lives still seem an enigma: how, we wonder, did they manage the physical difficulties of such a life? What kind of relationship must have pertained between them? But there is still a more interesting question: in what ways did they know their island and how did they experience it?

I take it as a given that Nan and Art Kellam knew their island; they explored the land by foot and the surrounding waters in their small rowing dory. While the world no doubt saw the edge of their island, Placentia, as a limiting boundary, they may have seen, with Heidegger, that "A boundary is not that at which something stops, but [rather] that from which something begins its presencing." They literally cleared a place for their own settlement and lodging; they created "presence."

And they wrote accounts of their discoveries. In a moving book titled *They Were An Island*, writer Peter Blanchard mined the Kellam's diaries and letters in the attempt to understand what appeared, at least superficially, to be solitary lives. Having decided to give up their lives in California, where Art Kellam was an engineer, the couple had explored various remote spots, some islanded and some not, in which to create a life for themselves. Their specific motivation is not clear; they appear not to have shared the mind set explored in books like Louise Dickinson Rich's (1942) *We Took to the Woods* or the accounts by Helen and Scott Nearing who popularized the back to the land movement in the 1960's.

The isolation/insular trope immediately leaps up of course in Peter Blanchard's title; the Kellams can be read as searching for an uncontaminated world, seeking out the farthest, smallest, most isolated island in which to live their ideal life. But viewed in another–and I believe more accurate–way, Blanchard suggests a close identification of the couple with the place they chose to inhabit: they *were* the island; in anthropologist Ingold's terms, they truly "dwelt" on (or perhaps we should say, *in*) their island. They worked, they built, they created, they explored. They moved in their space.

And they were sensitive to the power of metaphor as well. An appealing lyricism marks Art's observation that "The island looked best from far enough out so that just the occasional points could be seen, with the rest of the shore dimming back in the fog. Each of the points then became a small vignette of trees and rocks, never before seen that way and strangely changeful as we moved along [in the dory]." The trees and rocks tell a "vignette" readable to the island observer who is him/herself also of an ever-changing landscape.

Kathleen Dean Moore has told us that in living on a small island, "you are fully attentive to the time and place. Once you start paying attention, you begin to see how extraordinary the place really is–beautiful, mysterious, contingent, surprising." Hardly scientific observers of the natural world in which they lived so intimately, the Kellams were people who nonetheless "paid attention": they discovered the "beautiful, mysterious, contingent and surprising." "Surprises," Blanchard notes, "were embedded in everyday experience." Together, the Kellams made new discoveries, whether a park-like wood, or an old trail that was the remnant of a nineteenth-century farm road.

And always, there is as well the view outward. As for other island habitants and writers, Placentia is a lens for viewing a larger world. In a 1953 journal entry, Nan writes: "Shades of blue in the sunlit water harborward–greys toward the sisters [Sister Islands]. Mountain on the Big Island (Mount Desert) like tremendous waves rising in succession from the sea and caught at the moment of greatest depth just before breaking . . . . A lone lobster boat returning from beyond Black Island." In Nan's descriptive lens, a large, perhaps violent, ocean is juxtaposed to a small lobster boat. Just as new perceptions may cancel out previous knowing, small things come to mean large. For those available to see them, the small island throws into relief the vagaries of scale.

Particularly in Nan's journal entries, "paying attention" is allied with an almost child like sense of discovery. It is no surprise that Nan Kellam tended to portray herself as a child, even "fairy child." Such depictions of self may have served various needs for Nan, and for a contemporary reader, they raise obvious questions about her relationship to her husband. Even on a remote island, the gender relations of a time–the 1950's and 60's– and culture were apparently present. But I see as well in Nan's self-styled fairy child persona an open-ness to the world that she and Art both created. If in one sense they "were" an island–in that they lived by themselves in an islanded place–they also undertook on Placentia Island a journey that enabled them to acquire a growing and profound knowledge of the world about them. The cover of Peter Blanchard's book on the Kellams shows the couple in their small but stout rowing dory. They seem at ease, almost drifting in a misty sea. But they know where they are going, which taxi to take; and they are probably not in a hurry.

CHANGING PLACES

I'm looking out the kitchen window to a scene that seems unchanged over more than forty years. There, in front of me, is our own field, then the neighbor's field, then the white fenced cemetery, and beyond that, the sweep of the island studded bay. As ever on a clear day, the Camden Hills in the far distance define the horizon. Yes, there are a few new–that is, less than forty years old–houses scattered around the island; but they are not many, and I do not see them from my window.

Nor does anyone approaching the island's pool and dock see them. If you've been coming to Gotts Island for, say, the last four decades, the approach looks pretty much the same. And we like it that way. Last summer a conversation among the island property owners about removing Uncle Mont's old cottage that guards the entrance to the dock revealed deep differences of opinion: the self-styled realists wanted the house torn down as decrepit and beyond repair; others (like myself) felt that such a drastic change, a sudden vacancy, would alter too dramatically that first view of the island, the island we "have always had."

I've been thinking about how we experience change differently according to where we are. While my aim is to know and describe an island where change, at least superficially, is relatively slow, for the writers in an anthology titled *West of 98* (the 98th meridian), change, the transformation from rolling prairie or plains to super markets and shopping malls is considerably more present, profoundly affecting the lives of those who live with it.

The work of writers who interrogate how Western landscapes, as William Kittredge says, "trigger" the imagination, are the more valuable to me because of the different time perspective they offer. Gotts Island is my "triggering" place in part because I can see virtually the same view from my kitchen window summer after summer. The writers describing their sense of the West, by contrast, have seen stark physical change within their own lifetimes: the physical environment looks, and is, very different from what it was in their childhood or youth. Given the age of many of the contributors to the anthology, that period is about forty to fifty years.

Gotts is a summer island, perhaps too small and remote, too unimportant, to have attracted major change. There is no land available for development, and with no easy deepwater access, the island holds little appeal for the wealthy yachting crowd. Gotts has been a seasonal island since the late 1930's. Any population growth, if one could call it that, results not from new people coming in, but from succeeding generations of the original summer families. Much of the newer building on the island is the result of a family's adding structures to their property to accommodate children and grandchildren.

A summer island like Gotts has its own kind of change of course: more outboards in the pool, all terrain vehicles supplanting the old wheelbarrows, cell phones and computers making communication with the mainland no longer a challenge, septic systems that meet Maine's environmental requirements, and solar panels bringing at least limited electricity to most of the houses. More significant still is the changed use of the island by the summer families. With the transformed economy of the middle-class family, with dual career parents, neither with much vacation time, gone is the old practice of mother and children (and to a much lesser degree, father) repairing to the family summer home the day after school lets out in June and returning the day before Labor Day. The coming and going, one could say nomadic, life of the summer islander now tends to involve short chunks of time, snatched from an otherwise busy, work-dominated life. Though I am also a nomad, a transient, on this island, ours is one of a small number of households that remain in residence all summer long. Very few children now–and this includes my own grandchildren, who live in Texas–spend more than a week or perhaps two on Gotts Island. What this means for the future remains to be seen.

So yes, I admit change, at least of a kind. But I'm still thinking about visible change in the physical environment; and why, though I recognize important shifts in our lives there, the island remains for me a quasi-permanent lens through which I experience the world–and write, My lens does not offer up change in the ways that the writers in the Western anthology describe.

"Maybe it's because I'm looking at the sea, which also seems, at least superficially, to be changeless."

I'm talking to John, my husband. He writes about the sea and its shores, and those who, throughout history, have lived their lives with them. As a historian, he will have no truck with de-historicizing the sea: "Just think how different it would have looked with many more fishing boats, and all with sail. The sea is hardly changeless."

One can't argue about that, but as for those boats under sail, that was really a long time ago, almost a hundred years. Ditto those small cottages and shacks that once lined the shore, as well as most of the large nineteenth-century houses that comprised the old village. I know they were there; the foundation holes remain, reminders of the once stalwart structures that I can see in old photographs of the original Gotts Island community. That was also the time before the spruce took over the open fields, devouring many signs of past habitation.

So I cannot deny physical change or the degree to which, as the inhabitant of one of those old houses, I live with fragments of the past. I recognize too that those remnants of pastness, integrated into my life, prove integral in constructing my own narrative of the island as place. It's just that I did not myself experience—as these Western writers apparently did—drastic change in what I see on the island: I came too late for that. That past captured in the photographs had already passed. The damage, one could say, had already been done.

The rapid and more recent change that characterized much of the West offers the memoirist a yardstick with which to measure change in her/his own life. The writer and the physical environment share a particular historical moment, both changing as it were, in tandem. And like the immense landscape that extends toward a great beyond, time also stretches out in a linear mode, encouraging what one writer calls a certain "fluidity" of self.

Time and change have a different valence on a small island. The island eludes linearity, its pace and rhythm of change enabled by two contrasting elements: land and sea in perpetual, and changing, conversation, both speaking across a border that changing with every moment of every day, is both fluid and porous. I see in the interaction between stone and sea not the "austerity" that writer Gretel Ehrlich has experienced in the granite of the western mountains she knows so well, but rather a motion that reflects my own transitory state, my own coming and going, given form in the repeated tidal rhythm of disappearance and return.

This does not mean that the island, the site of a lost nineteenth-century fishing and farming culture, is a place where a distant past can be preserved, whatever nostalgic wish we might have. Uncle Mont's old and increasingly derelict red cottage is a case point. On the one hand, I side with those neighbors who are firmly against the removal of a structure that, at least in everyone's memory, has always stood, an iconic presence, by the dock. I want, with my friends, to see the island remaining the "way it was." But at the same time, I know that such imagined fixity–even if possible–is not enough, the picture incomplete without the sea and its ever moving tides that beat in just a few yards away from the door of the old cottage. What seems fixed needs its other, each an element in a continually fluctuating relationship.

Linear time is not enough in this place. It is not enough for me and does not enable the stories I want to tell.

3

QUARRIES

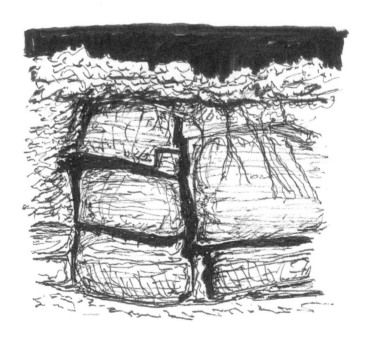

"[S]tories . . . [work] their way to the surface of the imagination."

PHILIP CONKLING
(INTRODUCTION, *HURRICANE ISLAND: THE TOWN THAT DISAPPEARED*)

It's hard to get away from stone on an island in Maine; and this is particularly true on a quarrying island. But Maine writer and environmental activist Philip Conkling sees more in this picture. He draws an analogy between the phenomenon of rocks rising slowly to the surface of a New England landscape and the generation of stories in a place whose history depended in good measure on the quarrying of stone. Conkling speaks too of imaginative quarrying, the kind we engage in as well when we come upon an old property deed, photograph or letter retrieved in a creaking drawer; a published record that strikes a particular personal chord; or, perhaps, a tale that circulates for generations in rumor or gossip. Island communities, even those existing in remnants, are also quarries of life stories, accounts of those who preceded us that wait to be unearthed from the past, pondered, and given life in new form.

In visiting two island quarries, both long disused, I ask what has been lost over the decades of human time; but also, what, if anything, can be exhumed from the past in stories that "work their way to the surface." Abandonment marks these islanded sites. Great chunks of granite, as well as dressed stone that was once intended for a post office building project in Chicago, Philadelphia or New York, bespeak an industry long gone. Enormous untrimmed blocks of stone make starkly visible a geological past even as they mark the disappearance of a human community. Rock torn from its primordial origin reminds us of the small place we ourselves occupy in the vast spectrum of time.

And yet, in their various forms, our stories endure.

VISITING THE STONE

Hurricane Island, 2005

All of us on the boat going out to Hurricane Island that day had read the history of the island: my husband and I, and also the tanned and sturdy young Outward Bound staffers who were our hosts. Until the program on Hurricane ended in 2007, it was their job to offer teenagers the opportunity to build self-reliance, teamwork skills, and other virtues through experience in the natural world.

It was unclear what role the history of Hurricane Island played in the adventure these youngsters were embarked upon. For Hurricane was hardly a site of unalloyed nature; it was a quarrying island. In the latter part of the nineteenth century it had housed a community of some 1500 people, who in a matter of days had been dislocated when an industrial operation and everything connected with it came to an abrupt end. Probably the teenagers, when they first arrived at the island, were as startled as we were; but would they see the human element in this apparently remote and deserted place where time and nature have held sway for a hundred years?

For us, of course, being well beyond teenage, the history recounted in Eleanor Motley Richardson's small book, *Hurricane Island: The Town that Disappeared*, was required reading. We wanted to know the human history of this place and had come in part to understand the meaning of loss and disappearance within time. The book was for us a map. Historical facts, clearly expressed, provide a picture to be savored and considered. They are also a lens that both frames and guides our experience of place. The human history of Hurricane Island colors and changes the so-called natural world that the Outward Bound youngsters were intended to encounter; the two are inextricably linked. But if a text, a history, can supply meaning to a natural site, what we accept as the "truth" of the text depends in turn upon our experience of that place. It is the interconnection between the physical, so-called natural, world and human history that so marks Hurricane Island. Perhaps this was the lesson that Outward Bound intended, ultimately, to impart.

That said, no text can adequately prepare the visitor for the visual experience of Hurricane: the vastness, within the relatively small space–roughly 150 acres–of the island, the major quarry with its towering cliff face, deep pond and borders of huge rough granite blocks tumbled about like a giant's playthings. The contrast in scale between the circumscribed space of a small island and the enormity of its features was almost overwhelming. The blocks of granite, tossed with seeming abandon, appeared to have erupted from the earth itself. But of course that was not the case. Human hands and energy created these fragments, some monstrous, some scaled to human proportion. Not far from the cliff face, stony rectangles identified the houses of the past and gave hint of former streets and lanes. Rocks protruded upward like druidic remains. A rusty boiler sat sedately in a grove of spruce, another unearthed remnant of the quarrying enterprise. This island, where a community worked and lived their lives, hacked out livings for almost fifty years, is a place of the blemished and the incomplete.

Like all essentially uninhabited islands, Hurricane is pervaded by an aura of remoteness in both time and space. Its history is not dissimilar from that of many of Maine's thirty-three granite-quarrying islands. Standing higher than its counterparts with a core that has been called a "mountaintop" in a valley depressed below sea level by the glaciers ten thousand years ago, Hurricane had never supported permanent settlement: a shell heap and arrowheads give evidence of earlier, seasonal occupants, but only one foundation and well pre-date the granite quarrying epoch.

The "deeper stories" that Philip Conkling found on Hurricane all date from the days of the quarrying community. These were the stories that in his words "work their way to the surface of the imagination." Here was a small lilac grove still blooming to life and a network of wells and drainage channels that revealed a complex water works system. In the deepest interior of the island, contrasting with the industrial archaeology of the massive granite works along the southern shore, were the remains of "motions": scores of small granite outcrops that had been worked by single individuals for paving stones.

Hurricane Island was purchased in 1870 for $50 by a retired Civil War general named Tilson who had fought at

Bull Run and earned the reputation of "petty tyrant." In 1877, the history tells us, some 255 workers were engaged in quarrying the granite used for post offices as far apart as St. Louis, Missouri, and Fall River, Massachusetts. How, exactly, they arrived in Maine from countries such as Ireland, Scotland, Finland, Italy, and Sweden, is not clear; and their actual numbers varied according to work available: in the decade 1875-1885, from 400-1000 men were employed. On the coast of Maine as a whole, the business of granite employed more men than fishing and farming combined. Small Hurricane Island boasted its own post office, bank, pool hall, bowling green, bandstand, ice pond, and ball field. The island was ostensibly dry, but a ship named Dark Secret carried a floating bar.

In 1880, 40,000 cubic feet of granite left Hurricane destined for the Washington Monument; the next year, 5000 tons of paving stone went to Chicago. In 1894 Hurricane granite was transformed into the pillars at Penn Station in Philadelphia, and in 1909 into the post office in St. Louis. A plethora of facts tell a history of this place, of huge urban monuments that stand in stark contrast to a now almost deserted small island. Worlds, and times, collide. So much of this place is out of place: in a clearing in the dim woods a carved section of pediment that never made it to that library or city hall in Boston or Milwaukee keeps silent vigil as a mnemonic of the past. How ironic it was that due to its remote and demanding location, this small island that once played its role in American city-building, was now offering strategies for survival in the natural world, to middle-class youth from the suburbs of those same cities.

Having finished lunch in the large dining area with the Outward Bound crew we set off to walk the circumference of Hurricane. We found a burial site and a small stone that marked the grave of an infant who was once part of a population of about 500 people. The name on this stone was fading into illegibility, but its message was clear. We had learned, from the book, that of fifty-two recorded deaths on Hurricane between 1892 and 1914, eighteen were infants or very small children. We walked on, followed the island's granite boundaries. We were moving in a silent world, Ozymandian in its intensity. Now out of range of the voices of the Outward Bounders, silence replaced the sounds that would once have turned the island into a Valhalla of industrial production, the blasting that Richardson says "happened about once an hour during the day and once every two minutes after 4pm when it was certain that everyone was out of the way." I tried to imagine that sound and the air filled with sticks and stones thrown up by the blasts.

Economic and industrial changes taking place far from the island and yet totally integral to its history brought sudden emptiness and silence to Hurricane. By 1914, concrete was replacing granite for major building projects, and times were hard for the Hurricane Granite Company. The death, from typhoid, of the company's able superintendent sealed the fate of the enterprise. A stark history was playing itself out. We could understand such change, but it was so much harder to grasp the suddenness of the ending and what it must have meant for those who lived through it. The incredible noise, the drilling, blasting, and polishing just stopped. The entire giant machine that was the quarrying operation came to a halt: like a sudden or accidental death. The workers and their families were left emptied of lives and livelihood. Furniture was left, pictures remained on the walls, tables left as set for the next meal that was not to be. In a matter of a few days, hundreds of people left on departing boats. Later, the houses were taken down and sold; the church pew, organ and altar went to the Catholic church on nearby North Haven Island. And not too long after that, General Tilson, the wealthiest man in Rockland–nearest large mainland port to Hurricane Island–was encased in his self-designed, entirely granite tomb.

It didn't take long to complete the circuit of Hurricane and return to the remains of the village and the cliff face of the quarry. And here we came upon new activity. One of the Outward Bound students was carefully descending the cliff, an ant-like figure on the rope, traversing the stone face on which, in 1877, an unskilled quarryman worked for $1 a day. Other students grouped themselves above and below, watching with quiet attention. No one spoke. The task required confidence, skill, and concentration.

In the trees to my right sat the gracefully curving, carved fragment of the pediment that never was, a flawed remain standing guard among the spruce. The young man continued his descent, further, slowly, painstakingly. Time crept on, the shadows growing gradually longer on the curving stone. Mesmerized, we continued to watch the man on the rope, breathlessly awaiting the denouement of this drama.

But we were not to see that final scene. Islands, and time, impose their own discipline, and we were after all short-term visitors in this strange and now silent place. It was time to make our way back along the trail to the dock. We had come to the island, and we had witnessed a site, a history, and a young man descending what was once a quarry face. Now all that remained was to board the boat for the journey back to the mainland.

Black Island, 2015

"Do you know where we can find the path to the quarry?"

The family piling out of their moored boat into a zodiac for the short row to the island seemed to know where they were going. Perhaps they could give us advice.

"Somewhere over there," came the shouted reply. The father of the family pointed in the direction to which we were also heading.

We had just rowed over from neighboring Gotts Island in our ten-foot skiff. We hadn't been on Black Island in years and had never seen the quarry. The received wisdom on Black was that the old path, which followed the original steam engine track, had become an impenetrable wilderness. It had not been used for almost a hundred years.

Black is another of Maine's old quarrying islands. It's the site of yet another deserted village, this one with hardly a trace of human habitation remaining. The faded photograph in Charles McClane's *Islands of the Mid-Maine Coast* shows a community gathered close to the shore on which we will soon be landing. But it is with only the greatest stretch of the imagination that we can envisage that group as people living and working in this place.

We had come to see the old quarry. We had been told that the Maine Coast Heritage Trust, which now holds an easement on the eastern side of Black Island, had cleared and marked the old trail; the quarry was now accessible. On a full tide, we pulled up our small boat beside the considerably larger zodiac on a narrow pebbly beach that barely accommodated us both. On our right a natural granite shelf sloped down to the sea; to our left was the high remainder of what was once a rocky wharf: the end point of the railway that brought down the stone for loading on to the barges headed for the mainland. The two Black Island quarrymen who drowned and were buried anonymously in the Gotts Island cemetery in 1896 must have begun their ill-fated journey here.

Having tied up the boat, we saw before us a cleared area and the blue blazes marking the now open trail. The MCHT had done their job well. We passed first the remains of an old stone cistern, then a few scattered vestiges of village habitation. The path was leading gradually up hill, an easy walk of less than half a mile. Though little evidence remained at this point, we knew we were on the old rail bed.

The zodiac family, who had lingered by the shore, were now somewhere far behind us on the trail, their voices lost in the stillness as we continued our ascent up the trail's gentle slope. Soon we saw chunks of rock, scattered remnants of the quarrying enterprise now lying forgotten in the woods flanking our path. A sepulchral quiet settled around us.

The geographer JB Jackson once wrote that stone, synonymous with duration, symbolic of origin and of cosmic order, lost its "sanctity" when, in columns and pilasters it celebrated human presence and scale. But what, then, do we make of this abandoned quarry that we have now come upon? Here surely, in an industrial ruin, is a human presence. Great piles of huge blocks of granite cut and blasted from the natural rock surround us. But unfinished as they are, left to stand on a small deserted island, in the very space from which they have been taken from the ground, these enormous structures–if we can call them that–seem, rather, to occupy a margin between the "cosmic" and the human. We see here no fragments of columns or pilasters like those we had seen at the much larger Hurricane Island. These blocks, cut by human hand and machinery though never used, stacked, perhaps for eternity, in piles more than fifty feet high, belong to a category of their own. We may imagine we are looking at some ancient temple ruin, but these huge higgledy-piggledy stacks, monumental in scale, suggest as well what Jackson would have called the "sanctity" of the primordial. They return us to geological origin even as they mark a lost world of human activity and place in sharp relief the insignificance of human time.

In our small skiff, it had taken about forty-five minutes of strenuous rowing to reach Black Island. Certainly not a long time, but we still felt we had embarked on an expedition, undertaken with all that one does not know–particularly weather and strength of the tide–about such journeys, however short. We had passed close to the salmon pens on the western end of the island, and moving easterly, had glimpsed the one house on the island, built by a summer family but on that day apparently uninhabited. When we came upon the family group in the zodiac we viewed them as fellow adventurers. We had all come to a relatively inaccessible place. We were out in the sea, out of current time.

It is something of a truism to speak of small, particularly uninhabited, islands as existing in a time of their own. Maine poet Ruth Moore once observed that such islands "live in their own sea." We tend to experience them as "out there," frozen in time. The fragments of past human habitation, the rocks torn from the quarry site, appear as elements in a static collage, framed by their island setting. On the one hand, then, exerting a power we do not feel in abandoned quarries on the mainland or on islands with year-round populations, they signal a bulwark against time; but in their very incompleteness, they suggest as well the transitory nature of the human hands that cut them from their natural setting. So we make our journey to bear witness, to mark, within this space of clashing time frames removed from more usual measures, our own place.

But this journey, like most, will end with a return to the reality of time that is ever in motion. As we re-enter the familiar Gotts Island outer pool the tide has changed and is running strongly against us. The receding waters push us back, and only by keeping as close to the shore as possible can we keep the skiff moving forward. This is the known, the expected cycle of things. Out on Black Island, the little beach where we tied up our boat will be high and dry by now, completely transformed. Like us, the zodiac family will have come and gone. But at the quarry, removed from such flux, the rocks still stolidly sit watch in the quiet woods.

GOOD AND LAWFUL DEEDS

"What with friends and family, I'm planning to use my house on the island this summer, so it won't be available for renting – this, unless it is sold. I've had a couple of offers for it, and am teetering."

As broadly hinted in her letter of February 1958, Ruth Moore, who chronicled the history of Gotts Island in both poetry and fiction, did indeed "teeter." Only ten days later, she wrote Phyllis and Richard Strauss, my sister and brother-in-law, that she would accept their offer for her Gotts Island house and its seventeen acres. "[A]s you know, I love the place," she explained; "[but] it's too much house for one; actually, it needs a big family, lots of kids running through it, which it will have if you buy it; so I don't feel too regretful." And by mid-April, in a warm letter in which she invited the new buyers to stay with her and her partner Eleanor Mayo, she informed them: "You're hooked now. I've cashed your check. I'm now hunting geography books for a safe place to abscond to."

Ruth Moore may have been ambivalent about selling her family home on Gotts Island; in an important sense, selling the property was part of losing the island culture into which she was born. Yet the letters to the young Massachusetts family who were purchasing the house as summer property reveal only mild regret, and Moore appears satisfied with the bargain she has struck. It was a similar story years earlier, in 1936, when, on the eve of her departure for a job in Berkeley, California, she was clearly the moving force in negotiating, on behalf of numerous family members, the sale of the Enoch Moore property to the daughter of a well-off Philadelphia Quaker family. There too, she seems eager to have the deal completed. In a letter to her mother published in Sanford Phippen's valuable collection, *High Clouds Soaring, Storms Driving Low: The Letters of Ruth Moore*, she wrote, "I hope to the Lord everything has gone through and that you folks have got your money . . . . I'm writing Uncle Bert, telling him to get the thing through as quick as he can."

The woman of these letters sounds so real, almost cheerily attending to the business of transferring ownership of a property. The physical document written for a specific audience also spells reality, though seemingly contained in time and in space. It does not tell us much of the historical surround, of the demise of Gotts Island's original, year-round population and the transformation of the island into a summer community. These events, typical of many Maine islands, are probed more deeply in Ruth Moore's prose fiction and poetry. Even her own departure from the island years earlier, seems, at the time she wrote to the Strausses, no longer a dominant issue. She and Eleanor Mayo had been settled in Bass Harbor (then called McKinley) for almost a decade by then.

But nothing is really contained, free of its context. A letter that was written to the Strauss family asserted a particular connection with them, its intended addressees; but it speaks a different message to me, an unintended reader who comes along fifty years later. Like time itself, the letter eludes stasis. The letters from Ruth Moore that my sister has recently given to me all ostensibly concern the purchase of the Philip Moore house in 1958; seven years later there would be other letters, these from my sister and brother-in-law to my husband and me: another transfer that renders to history the agreement negotiated in the earlier correspondence. All these letters reify transition, changes in and through time; reading them in the present connects us with the past, with negotiations long completed, with intentions that may or may not have been fulfilled.

Old property deeds, like the letters, are also markers of change. They codify histories of ownership, connect us with those earlier owners now departed and long gone. But because the past is so often what historian David Lowenthal has called a "foreign country," the truths that the old deeds so authoritatively enunciate appear illusory when read in a later context. The document has lost its original authority; the departed owner is the master or mistress of no property. History has an authority of another kind.

True to her calling as historian of Gotts Island, Ruth Moore knew this when she began a poem calling our attention to the "first deed":

> This is a copy of the first deed,
> Written two hundred years ago
> ("To Have and Not To Hold")

I have never seen the "first deed" through which Daniel Gott, in 1789, acquired the island that was later to be called Gotts Island, in what is now the state of Maine. And when Ruth wrote these lines in a poem published in the 1990 collection titled *The Tired Apple Tree*, I don't know if she had actually seen that first early document. But I do know that she wants us to imagine it:

> In the graceful and beautiful handwriting of that time.
> It [the first deed] is heavy with the language of law
> But it leaves no loopholes,
> And it speaks for itself now,
> As if a single bell-note, struck so long ago,
> Had sounded through the centuries unchanged.

The deed is "heavy with the language of the law." It speaks "for itself," it "leaves no loopholes." But the document that at first appears so solid and unchanging, so verifiable ("This is a copy"), soon turns otherwise: the deed can only speak *as if* its authority would sound "unchanged" through the centuries. Of course, as the poet/historian well knows, change will come. "Having," as the poem's title indicates, is not "holding." The first stanza of the poem, framing what is to come, suggests that the authority of the legal deed is in some sense no authority at all.

The so-called historical and geographical facts only reinforce the illusion of immutability: a committee empowered by the Commonwealth of Massachusetts has sold to Daniel Gott for eighteen pounds what is now Great Gott and Little Gott Islands. We know how many acres Daniel purchased and where exactly the property is located. But despite the language–"The said Commonwealth shall warrant and defend the said Premises to him, / His Heirs and Assign forever, /Against the lawful claims of all persons whatever"–the point of the poem is that the Gotts and the Moores, as well as the other island families, would not hold the island forever. A longer view of the history of Gotts Island reveals the fragility of ownership, both for them and for those who would come after them.

Ruth must have been well aware when she wrote the letters to the Strausses in 1958 that in the larger context, the transferral of the property was yet another sign of Gotts Island's having become a summer habitat for people from away. Perhaps that's why it seems so important to her to turn the business at hand, the legalities of the sale, into an exploration of the history of the house. Over and over, Ruth moves into the past to reactivate the old owners, the ghosts who still lodge there, questioning the validity of any modern legal deed and the notion of ownership itself.

The chief vehicle of Ruth's exploration of past history is the original deed through which Daniel Gott transferred what became the Moore property to his son Nathaniel. Nathaniel's daughter Asenath would later marry the first Captain Philip Moore, thereby linking the Moore and Gott families. This is a deed that I also know. It is framed on the living room wall of our Gotts Island house, the spidery script becoming ever more faint. I can hardly decipher the writing now, but Daniel's signature is legible, as is the "mark"–the X–of his wife Hannah. "Hannah, her mark" the writing below the faded X still reads. The date is 1812. Two years later Daniel and two of his other sons were drowned while fishing near Mount Desert Rock.

For Ruth Moore, this is the deed that counts. It has no legal value, its authoritative language, like that of Daniel Gott's "first deed," irrelevant; but Daniel's signature and Hannah's faded mark, encoded within the old document, have a permanence that transcends their actual lives. In this sense, the original owners of the property belong *to* the house even if the property on which the house sits no longer, in a legal sense, belongs to them. Or perhaps, as I prefer to think, the house, in another sense, does belong to them: they are still presences here.

The 1812 deed that calls up these presences dominates Ruth Moore's correspondence with the Strausses in 1958, appearing in three separate letters. Ruth was planning to give this deed to the new buyers, and she seemingly wanted them to understand that because it recognizes, even pays homage to, the ghosts that still populate the island, its value exceeds that of the actual legal document at hand. The old deed, the letters suggest, is a good deed. As described in Ruth's letter of February 12, 1958, "Grandfather Gott," "Clarence Turner," "Jack Gott," as well as information regarding changes to the original house–all are here:

> I have, somewhere, the original deed to [the house], where the original grandfather Gott deeded this particular portion of his estate to his son, so I think the title's clear. . . . father bought it from Clarence Turner around 1900, and Clarence Turner from Andrew (Jack) Gott. The original house, I understand, (the part over the cellar) was rebuilt and added to because one of the old ladies got mad because her kitchen windows didn't look out over the water. I don't know which family this was. Berl [Berlin Gott] could have told you–and it's partly legend, anyway.

It seems hardly to matter what is legend and what is not. All is of equal value and significance. Two months later, with a light touch that ostensibly distances herself from the history, Ruth again alludes to the old deed, now connecting it with the long history of the Moore family:

> I enclose "Great-Grandfather's Deed." I think perhaps he may have been my "Great- grandfather's" Great-Grandfather, but am not sure. I've never dug around much in the ancestors, fearing I may come

> up with the one who was hanged for stealing a sheep.

It's as if she cannot let the old deed go. But since she is actually having to let go of it and what it stands for, she needs to stress its importance.

> The land was, I believe, a part of Daniel Gott's original purchase, and I have the original deed to it, signed by him, in which he made this particular portion over to his son. You can have this deed, if you want it, along with yours; not that you need it, but it's nice to have.

"Not that you need it," she says of the old deed. But of course they "need" it. And so, I think, does Ruth. The old deed has special value not as an inert document but as malleable material that endures, albeit with changed relevance, over time. As archaeologist as well as historian, Ruth Moore was well aware that against time itself, especially geological time, a document of ownership per se has no power. This is the message of three poems–of which "To Have But Not to Hold" is the second–published in *The Tired Apple Tree* collection. Together, the poems take us from pre-history up through the modern period: from molten rock to real estate.

Within the long perspective, the land is always larger than any footprint, or boundary, that human settlement–or ownership—may place upon it. "The rocks of the earth are its history/[and] They tell what's known of who got here first,/They say how old is old," the first poem, titled simply "Rocks," begins. But, it is implied, we do not hear or attend to the language uttered by the rocks; we are essentially ignorant of the "secret ebb and flow/Or what roared over the earth's crust/Billions of years ago." Not understanding that far distant history within which we ourselves play no role, we cannot imagine a world not defined as property.

"The Offshore Islands," the third poem in the sequence, brings us into human time and more specifically, to a thumbnail history of Gotts Island that recapitulates a story so often repeated on Maine's islands. This poem begins also with the land before settlement:

> The offshore islands belong to themselves,
> They stand in their own sea.
> They do not inherit; they leave no heirs.
> They are no man's legacy.

Like the rocks of the earlier poem that evoke "Blazing volcanoes, cooled and dead" that "[m]arked nowhere a boundary line," the offshore islands, left to themselves, "leave no heirs" and "are no man's legacy." Notions of ownership of property, deeds, and written records will come only later. And with the arrival of this other history, the stages of development pass in dizzying succession. Following the Indians ("first summer people") came the permanent white settlers who "made fast [their] own boundary lines," and willed property to their sons. Then, with passing generations, this "pioneer" community "felt the mainland's pull" and "abandoned their homes to rot away." The stage is set for the final, and worst, period: the "era of real estate, /Of the hundred thousand dollar lots, / Of the condominiums, side by side, /Along the shoreline choicest spots." As for the future, it is as unclear to us as the far distant archaeological past– "What follows the time of developers/No human voice can tell."

A calculus of ownership dulls the ear and blurs the vision. It creates an alienated past in which we cannot see or hear the ghosts who have become mere deed and boundary makers, transient actors at odds with the "silent" knowledge that the islands eternally hold. But those ghosts, Ruth says, "have never gone away." Rather, they endure within the silence for those willing to recognize them. They inhabit spaces like the old 1812 deed, which by 1958 was no longer about property but had become, rather, a vessel containing the traces of the lives of people living in relation to place: "Hannah, her mark," Hannah's place.

Ruth's letters transform property into place. She is not so much selling a piece of bounded property to the Strausses as handing over to them a place. That's why, while attending to boundaries is requisite to the business of the sale, Ruth provides her own idiosyncratic mode of description. In a letter in March 1958 regarding a 1947 survey she writes:

> I have never been thoroughly satisfied with it [the old survey], I must admit, as it has always seemed to me to be a little off. Whether this is due to magnetic variation through the years or to the way the old folks measured up-hill and down-dale with a pole, I don't know. . . . As I remember, in my childhood, the "large spruce" marked on the boundary between Hilda Kenway and me, use to have a pole tied to its top to show that it was Babbidge's (now Kenway's) corner bound. . . . I never felt, however that the lines were enough off to make a fuss over. A few feet one way or the other, so what, except for a nice spot of cranberries which I always looted anyway.

If Ruth Moore has to talk about boundaries, she is going to do it in her own way. A large spruce, a remembered note about some earlier agreement with Hilda Kenway, and a patch of cranberries are more important than the exactness of the surveyor's rod. Similarly, the title search completed by Silsby and Silsby's law offices in Ellsworth has to be discussed, but is seemingly important to Ruth because it provides another occasion to move back into the history of the individuals who inhabited the place:

> They tell me there that forty years is generally considered far enough back for legal purposes in these parts, and as you will see they have carried the search back to 1901. . . . The land was, I believe, a

part of Daniel Gott's original purchase, and I have
the original deed to it, signed by him, in which he
made this particular portion over to his son.

Just as she tells the Strausses that she is leaving in the house the contents necessary to housekeeping–"probably most of that stuff ought to stay where it is anyway," she says–she implies that she is leaving them not inanimate objects but living material through which a real history can be grasped.

The quasi business correspondence is really about the "stuff" of the house and the "stuff" included in the old deed, those faded 150-year-old signatures that recall the past into the present. The boundary that matters is not the surveyor's iron pipe but a more vaguely defined patch of cranberries that has significance in the remembered life of the island. The cranberries and the spruce tree are the real. Ruth seems to be telling the Strausses in 1958, and telling me as well even now, that acquiring the Moore house and land means acquiring a past, both real and imagined. It's as if voices from another century, all the "inheritors," come with the property.

Ruth Moore's letters to the Strausses constitute in themselves a "good deed"; they are a gift that I, fifty years later, read as a form of instruction. No doubt, Ruth knew the challenge she faced in putting forth such a lesson. Fifteen years later, in a letter included in Sanford Phippen's collection, she wrote: "The last local people who went [to the island] for a Sunday outing were ordered off, since even shorelines now are mostly private." In 1989, less than a year before her death, she wrote movingly to my late neighbor, Betty Baldwin, herself a summer person whose friendship with the Moore family went back to the 1920's:

> Of course I'd love to see you any time, but you mustn't ask me to go to the Island. I haven't been down there for years, and have no wish to go. It's no longer the magical place I knew and loved and grew up in and the changes made set too many ghosts walking. (Jan, 1989)

Once again, an island turned into measured property is no longer open to the "magic," to the "ghosts" she knows are there. In a similar vein a year earlier, in a letter to Betty Baldwin's brother, Ted Holmes, also a close friend from long past summers on Gotts Island, Ruth remarked what she saw as the inhospitality of the summer people and then observed:

> It almost seems as if the people down there [on the island] were afraid of something. I wouldn't know what. I know it seems haunted to me. Not without reason. The offshore islands are mysterious, anyway; I've been on some of them where there once were villages, even towns, where there's a definite atmosphere, almost in the air, that no one is welcome there–that the island belonged to itself and always did (Feb. 13, 1988).

Then in her eighties, Ruth again looked to the islands that "speak with a voice that is all their own," are silent to modern generations, and continue to harbor ghosts of the past. Even as she clearly regretted the path she saw its history as having taken, the island still holds for her its special "atmosphere," the mystery that is its essential meaning.

Though a modern deed of ownership has little to say about them, the presences are still there. As Ruth Moore's letters to the Strauss family in 1958 suggested, there is in some sense no real departure. Something always remains, whether in Daniel Gott's faint signature–and Hannah Gott's X–on the old 1812 deed or in the mid-twentieth-century faded typescript that tells a story of its own. These documents are my inheritance also. The lessons are still there to be learned, the ghosts recognized, the silences heard, and the mystery woven into the fabric of our own lives.

DEPARTURE

In Maine they say that when you hear the crickets, it's six weeks to first frost.

Today, I walked in the field by the small cemetery where my son is buried, feeling the tall grasses, once soft and pliant, crackle stiffly under my feet. Today I heard the crickets for the first time.

Of course I will have left the island long before the frost comes. We summer islanders are always transients here, arriving in June with bag and baggage, departing in late August or early September with memories of the present year and lists of house tasks scheduled for the next one. John and I will walk down the hill once again, pause for a few moments by Ben's grave to say good-bye, look back at our house up on the hill—and then, once again, we'll be off.

The rhythm has gone on, year after year, decade after decade. I like to think that I remember all our arrivals and departures. But of course I don't. I can recall only the special ones, like the one that had to be postponed when a howling northeaster blew in the night before we were supposed to leave and a still-wild sea posed too much risk to the mail boat. The boys were still young then. I remember seeing the bags and boxes piled up by the kitchen door all ready for the trip "off" that had to wait until the next day.

All the departures are important, the coming–and the going–year after year. It's the rhythm that counts, that is so much part of what bonds us to this island.

I thought Ben would return when we said good-bye to him that July day so many years ago. We didn't know then that some departures are final, that sometimes the rhythm of departure and return is irrevocably broken. Pattern is all, an unexpected interruption so importantly a part of our loss. The only blessing perhaps is unexpectedness itself; we are spared the curse of foreknowledge.

The knowing, or the not knowing, makes such a difference. But when, then, is the knowing? Was it there in the tightness I felt in my stomach when Ben left for a strange and alien place on the other side of the globe? Did I in some way know that my son would die in a freak flying accident on an African savannah? If so, what kind of knowledge–or if not knowledge, at least awareness–is this?

It's now more than a month since Rose Atwood, my neighbor, left the island to spend the rest of her life in a nursing home. Like Ben, she will not return. But was there a terrible, even fearful, moment, before the dementia reached its more extreme stage, when Rose knew that the condition in her brain would force this departure? As it was, when she left for the nursing home she didn't seem to know that this trip would not be like the hundreds of others she had taken over the years, all those trips off that led always to a coming back: "coming on" as the old islanders say. If there was awareness, it could not be detected.

She can't walk easily now. When she left she had to be transported to the dock in the shiny red jeep that looks exactly the same as it did when purchased thirty years ago. Everything in the Atwood household is carefully, even obsessively, cared for. The jeep is no exception. But of course, it hasn't been driven very far. Where can you drive to on an island that is only one mile across with no real roads? The odometer registers less than 2000 miles, and 600 of those can be chalked up to the maiden trip from the dealer in New York.

All the Atwoods' shopping trips to the mainland begin the same way, the jeep making its way slowly along the dirt and sodded track that we call the town road. No one would drive full throttle on the town road, which passes like a narrow ribbon by the field that girds the cemetery. The passage of the red jeep, one of a kind on an island of few vehicles, is like that of a royal procession. Even on her last day on the island, Rose sat upright in the high passenger seat: like the pope or the queen.

The next day, Forrest, Rose's husband, offered us an electric mixer that he'd unearthed in clearing out the closets and cabinets in his wife's kitchen. He walked up the hill to our house, mixer in hand. It was just like the one we received as a wedding present in 1960 and later, in one of our many moves, gave up in a garage sale.

"I have a new one," he told us.

Forrest feels in control when he has the latest, and best, model of whatever appliance he owns. But I like my old hand beater that's done the job for more than forty summers. Even though we've just installed a modest new solar electricity system, a major event by any standard in a 140-year-old house on a remote island in the Gulf of Maine, we don't want electric appliances.

"It's an offer you can't pass up," Forrest said.

But we did.

"He'll have to get rid of her clothes too," a neighbor who happened to stop by later that day reported. "At the nursing home only four changes of clothes per season are allowed. No buttons or zippers."

I'm thinking of the clothes that would be allowed—pull-on pants with elastic tops, sweaters, tee-shirts, formless garments: the clothing of the old or those who, at least in the view of those who run nursing homes, are unaware or uncaring.

Rose's blue windbreaker, the one she always wore on the island, had a zipper. It must have been left behind. I wonder if the dementia wiped everything out or if Rose remembers her jacket and misses it. Oddly enough, I miss it. On a small island I can recognize everyone coming along the road by either clothes or walk. Even on a foggy day, I can identify a formless person in a blue or red jacket. And I can still see Rose in her windbreaker coming up the path with the mail, walking toward the kitchen door, past the garden where the poppies glow orange and red in July.

No weeds were ever allowed to grow in Rose's garden. The red currant bushes were perfectly maintained, the grass manicured. Nothing went untamed on the Atwood property. Long before the television shows that promoted the rehabilitation of old houses, the Atwoods had elevated reconstruction and maintenance to high art. While we continue to fuss, usually unsuccessfully, with leaking roofs, recalcitrant pumps, and cracking plaster, nothing at their house ever looks worn out, shabby, or old.

But all of the still-standing original island dwellings are old. Forrest bought his house from the Harris family soon after he came home from the war in 1946. The Harrises had been on the island for three generations but, like all the other year-round families, had moved off well before the war. It's what happened on scores of islands off the coast of Maine. At least in winter, they turned into ghost towns. Most of the houses fell down, victim to fire, rain, rot, and the weight of winter snow. Summer people saved what remained. Over five decades, Forrest and Rose made their house both weather-tight and, in their terms, "modern." They valued the history of their house of course, but the real point was to bring the property "up to date." And keep it that way.

Don't beat the cake batter by hand if you can use electricity. The Atwood house was the first on the island to have a generator and then a solar electric system, hot running water that didn't have to be run in copper tubing through the wood stove, even a television set. On a July night in 1969, the entire population of the island forced themselves to stay awake well past their normal bedtime, crowding around the Atwoods' then small screen to witness the moon landing. John always remembers that Rose, as proprietor of the tv set, sat in a rocker directly in front of the screen; and every time she rocked forward, the entire image was obliterated. I'm still wondering if I actually saw the "step for mankind."

Rose spent many summer weeks alone in the island house with her four children. Those were the years when Forrest was still selling construction equipment and had only two weeks vacation. She learned early on to manipulate all the elaborate systems that her husband installed in the house. She made sure that the boys kept the field around the house perfectly groomed. She made quarts of red currant jelly from the produce of the large bush behind the barn. She prepped and painted at a level few professional painters could attain, tore down old wallpaper and put up new. No tool or implement was ever out of place when the job was done. The barn, which serves as workshop as well as garage for the red jeep, was, and is, always immaculate, never a spot of paint or oil on floor or bench.

In its pristine whiteness, the house triumphs over the usual ravages of time and wear.

I always count time on the island in terms of summers. The events of winter are strangely distant here. The raw pain I felt when Ben died in that plane crash on Christmas Day had softened into a more subtly aching emptiness by July, when we buried his ashes in the island cemetery; and after that, we thought of all the summers as either "before" or "after." In our first summers on the island, John and I were the "young marrieds with children." Our first son was three months old when we brought him to the island for the first time and had to borrow an extra sweater from Rose and Forrest's daughter Susan, who was a year older. The infant who wore the borrowed sweater is now a father himself; and more than fifteen summers have passed since we brought to the island the simple slab of granite to mark Ben's grave.

The island is its own timeline. Everyone has a generational place. John and I have become the older generation. Forrest is almost the oldest of all. He came to the island as a child, traveling up from Boston with his family. They were at first summer boarders, and then his mother bought the house that shares the top of the hill with ours. That would have been about 1930, the year that meant the end for most of the full-time island people. Ultimately came the war, and then the opportunity to purchase island property for almost nothing. Forrest, a young veteran with little cash, was able to acquire a house of his own, and four years later a wife as well. He and Rose spent their honeymoon on the island in 1950 and embarked upon their never-ending round of home improvement.

The Atwoods, like everyone else on the island, have another house on the mainland, no doubt also well maintained. But none of us speaks much of our mainland, winter, houses. Home is the island, the place where imagination, no less than a house, can be fabricated and maintained. Once on the island there is no other place; everything else, like the nursing home on the mainland, away from the coast, belongs to the great amorphous sphere of the not-here.

"It's run by good people," Forrest, still holding the mixer, told us. "Rose will be happy there. She'll like the sociability. They even have a van to take the residents on little outings."

Perhaps we should have accepted that old mixer. It could, I suppose, have been a kindness, possibly helping Forrest get on with his life. But John and I didn't want to involve ourselves in that way. Not that we haven't taken on other objects that the Atwoods thought outdated and wanted rid of: the twin beds and mattresses that we put in our small guest room for instance, the old bathroom scale in the back hall bathroom. And years ago we made curtains for our homemade puppet theater with material that had once graced an Atwood bedroom.

No, we weren't against taking the Atwoods' cast-offs; but not the electric mixer, and not just then.

"Giving away the mixer means getting rid of the ghosts and the agony that drove him to put her in the nursing home," John said. No more dealing with the chaos of a failing mind and body. Adult diapers, all of that. Now everything can be tidy and orderly again. We couldn't judge Forrest's decision to take Rose to the nursing home; but we didn't want to be part of it. From a distance, the untidiness of old age seems tolerable.

Rose's dementia proceeded slowly, hardly noticeable at first and, as far as the rest of us could see, changing little from summer to summer. But then, how could we know the whole story? We did know that the island is no country for the old, that Forrest became increasingly anxious about leaving Rose alone in the island house, even if the errand ashore was to be brief. Two years ago, a visiting jogger found her, almost a mile from home, exhausted and confused, clutching a tree at the edge of a steep eroded bluff that hangs over jagged rocks and a pounding sea. Later, on a bitterly cold day in the winter, at their home on the mainland, she wandered out into the snow. The police were alerted. After a hunt of several hours, with wintry darkness falling, she was found resting peacefully in the house of a neighbor who had gone out and left the door unlocked.

Forrest knew that he had to have help on the island. When John and I arrived this summer on a brilliantly clear day with the wind from the southwest, we saw someone we didn't recognize hanging out sheets on Rose's clothes line. It was, as my mother always said, "a good drying day," but we had never before seen an Atwood guest hanging out the clothes; and having lived just up the hill for forty summers, we pretty well know what is usual and what is not.

But Evelyn, of course, was not a guest. A Peruvian and recent immigrant to Maine, Evelyn, accompanied by a small, observant six year old son, had been hired by Forrest to help care for Rose and to spend the summer on an island totally alien to her.

"As long as I have Evelyn I can keep Rose on the island for one more summer," Forrest told us. Evelyn was his last chance. He had come up the hill with little Daniel, Evelyn's boy, to help John move the sailboat, "Hint of Trouble," out of the barn where it had spent the winter. Daniel stood by his side, watching with dark intelligent eyes and a slightly mischievous smile, apparently enjoying the freedom offered by the island and the opportunity to help with "men's work."

But for his mother, the situation was clearly different. Evelyn was pleasant, willing and able. It all seemed like a good plan. But we weren't considering how difficult it must have been for a woman with limited English to live twenty-four hours a day on an island removed, except for her small son, from the rest of her family. It was only later, when a weekend on the mainland convinced her she couldn't go on with the job, couldn't return to the island, that we all wondered how Evelyn had lasted as long as she did. The brief chapter ended. There would not be "one more summer" for Rose.

Farewells, enacted year after year, have a special resonance on a summer island; "time to go," we say. I think once again of Ruth Moore's description of "compassionate summer" that only leases to us "[a] sheaf of days as beautiful and brief as bubbles, rising, breaking, in the sea." She knew, as I do not, the "first snow" that "flake by flake, creep[s] up the bending bough." She knew the frost prophesied by the crickets.

Though it seemed on the surface so ordinary, we didn't need the crickets to tell us that the farewell party that Forrest planned for Rose meant a special, out-of-time, kind of ending. The setting was the Atwoods' pink kitchen with the Sears and Roebuck oak cabinets. The room, like so many on the island, was frozen in time, changed little from the evening we had gathered to watch the moon landing. We knew it all so well. Even Rose looked the same, sitting in her customary place by the kitchen window that looked out across the field and to the bay beyond.

No one sat down. Rather, in standing, we seemed be waiting for something to happen, some climactic moment that was going to change everything. Conversation lurched awkwardly on, brittle and falsely bright. We felt that we were colluding in Forrest's decision, being asked to confirm its rightness, to make it irrevocable. We were conspirators in making Rose believe that this event was essentially no different from any neighborly gathering. But even more, we were being called to witness a kind of social death.

The only person who seemingly grasped none of this, who played, if we can call it that, her own authentic role, was Rose herself. That, surely, was the crucial point. Though apparently advanced into dementia, Rose was still in some uncanny way still the woman we all knew. There she sat with her usual good-natured self-confidence, responding cheerily to the comments of her guests.

Roles are inviolate on the island: everyone has their place. Rose's departure would mean a gap. There would be a space, most sadly and crucially for Forrest of course, but for the rest of us too. An acute sense of loss hung over our little gathering in the kitchen. We had known the deaths of old and young in our islanded summer world; but this liminal death–I can think of it only that way–was terrible perhaps because it was not entirely final but yet had the aura of finality. This quasi death underlined the concrete realness of loss even as it pointed up the ambiguity that inhered in the whole situation.

A real death leaves fewer unanswered questions. If it had been a funeral or memorial service, the ritual in the kitchen could have acknowledged the loss; but as it was, it had to fail. Rose's physical presence before us was too powerful. She seemed too much in touch with her surroundings, the social personality intact. The dementia, though always lurking beneath the surface, was masked. We wanted to believe it was not there, could almost believe it wasn't. It was easy to recognize the strong feisty woman who had learned easily to operate all the gadgetry that Forrest had installed in the house over the years, had, in the first year of their retirement, joined Forrest in wintering alone on the island, and most important, had researched and published a chronicle of all the island families. She spoke with an authoritative voice in that book; she positioned herself at the center of the island and its lore. She was the "island expert." As expected, some people resented that stance, but she was, in fact, more expert than most of us.

But we weren't thinking of that on the day of the impromptu farewell party. We were just trying to do what we could. We exchanged old stories and memories and current gossip. If Rose could sense the constraint, even sadness that sat behind the upbeat voices and light laughter, it was not apparent. She was making it easy for us to believe in her not knowing what this party was really about.

Pain is for those who know. It was apparent, though partially hidden behind false brightness, in Forrest's face. Susan, youngest child and only daughter, hiding her grief, remained silent. For the rest of us, it was a relief when the time came to bid the final farewells to the woman who didn't know she was leaving, to say good-bye in the way we would if we were planning to see her again the next day and all the summer days thereafter. The good-bye was the most poignant, and hence most difficult, part of the play we were enacting that day. Once uttered, we could jostle our way hastily out the kitchen door, through the barn, and into the late afternoon light.

On a small island like ours, everything happens on the high tide: all the arrivals and the departures depend on the level of water in the pool. Early the next morning, when I looked out my kitchen window toward the cemetery and

Ben's grave, I saw that the tide was coming in swiftly. I knew I would soon see the jeep, with its three passengers, make its way slowly down the hill toward the boat that was called Invincible. The jeep was loaded with the usual bags and tanks that anyone takes for a day of errands on the mainland. Rose would have thought it was like any other day, probably did not notice that a bag of her own clothing and personal objects was among the usual load. Neither would she have looked back to watch her house disappear from view as the jeep descended toward the sparkling blue water that rose, bubbling in its haste, around the dock.

The crickets were silent.

DESERTION

*"The path was a vague parting in the grass
That led us to a weathered window-sill.
We pressed our faces to the pane..."*

Robert Frost, "The Black Cottage"

The long-term summer islanders tell me that in the late 1940's and early 1950's the deserted houses, empty since about 1930 when the island was depopulated, were still standing. "I even saw old letters," one neighbor told me. She had been a child then. She recalled the delight of going into a derelict house, the signs of habitation still there. It could be dangerous; her mother had prohibited her playing there. But that was only another reason to go.

The summer children could "play house" in the deserted structures falling gradually into ruin. They could enter a past that was real in a concrete way, even slip into the lives created–or perhaps endured–there. They found in such play the seductive thrill of transgression: these houses, and the objects left behind, had belonged to others. And in a sense they still belonged to the ghosts whose lives could be called up again. No wonder that these children, even now approaching the end of their seventh decade, remember and recount their experiences so clearly.

Letters, artifacts of lives now gone, stand out in adult memory. But as children, my neighbors may not have felt the sad irony in reading words written years ago by people long gone, whatever personal matters contained therein never to be read in the same way. Perhaps only time and aging enable us to put the past into context, to recognize that the letter that once connected a particular and unique writer and reader now, in a far different way, connects us to lives lived in the past.

Geographer JB Jackson has asserted that the "ramshackle deserted house" may be seen as a "chrysalis from which [the] inhabitants have escaped to some brighter more alluring prospect." But alluring futures were not much on offer in 1930. Although the islanders who left their homes in a time of economic depression may have hoped for brighter prospects on the mainland, allure seems hardly the appropriate term. They left; they got on with their lives, some-–though a small minority–venturing as far afield as New York or even California (the building of San Francisco's Golden Gate Bridge in the mid-thirties summoned the member of one island family westward). Some thought they would return to the island for temporary summer visits, and some actually did. But most did not. About half a dozen families sold their houses to summer people, former holiday boarders. The rest of the old village houses fell derelict, providing enticement for the summer children a decade or so later.

Jackson's language of escape suggests that the inhabitants are finally and completely gone. For him, the derelict house as "chrysalis" represents a transitory state in a life trajectory. Desertion, emptiness, is total. But the island children did not find emptiness. And neither does Robert Frost, meditating on a deserted dwelling in "The Black Cottage." The distance between past and present is there of course. The first speaker tells us that he and his companion–the local minister who becomes the main voice of the poem–simply "chanced" to catch sign of the cottage "in a sort of special picture" among the trees, "set well back from the road." The minister "made as if to hold it [the cottage] at arm's length/Or put the leaves aside that framed it in": in framing the cottage, Frost underlines the gap between observer and observed object.

Like the children who explored the deserted frame houses on Gotts Island, the two sojourners in Frost's poem press their faces to the windowpane of the deserted cottage and see that "Everything's as she [the former occupant] left it when she died." Household objects enable narrative. A faded daguerreotype of the woman's husband recalls to the minister the woman's account of her husband's death in the Civil War. Then the sons had gone off–perhaps following the allure that JB Jackson describes–and the woman was left alone. The life story is not a happy one; but the passersby feel a more acute sadness from the realization that the "world has passed [the cottage] by," and the dwelling itself has become the "mark" of time: a "measure of how far fifty years have brought us."

Frost's poem is about time and what is permanent and what is not. Time has agency: "The warping boards pull out their own old nails/With none to tread and put them in their place." The house cannot withstand such processes. The typical American wood frame house, Jackson has suggested, was never expected to be physically permanent. Americans, in his view, are not drawn to permanence. But where he credits the American tendency to move on, leaving the house behind to fall to ruin, Frost and his narrator attend to the life that was lived in the small cottage and, even more important, the values that were essential to it: independence, resolution, devotion to ideals both spiritual and secular. The connections lie there. Frost places himself in a tradition that was attracted to structures in decay, to empty spaces and rooms that call up, imaginatively, the presence of the absent and, even, what could be called "New England values."

The near derelict cottage black with rain and sitting apart from a village, the old daguerreotype on the wall now faded with age, triggers for the poet Frost a discovery of what endures more broadly in both time and space, of the "truths we keep coming back and back to." Physical impermanence cannot be avoided: "Scattered oases where men dwelt, [are now] Sand dunes held loosely in tamarisk/Blown over and over themselves in idleness." The environment built or organized by human kind offers no protection against time and blowing sands. Permanent truths dwell in a world in motion. Frost offers us ultimately a stark oxymoron: what endures is witnessed in impermanence.

Robert Frost's poem on the deserted dwelling moves us far beyond the experience of those Gotts Islanders who were children sixty years ago. Or at least, as they were then. But here they are now, on a gray day on a small island in Maine, describing those houses to me. I am like the minister's companion; I want, and need, to know their story. They recount the names of the families who lived there–yes, those names are still remembered–and recall their own pasts in reference to that earlier generation. In some way it doesn't matter that so little is left of that physical community, that the derelict structure has now become, at best, a cellar hole and foundation. The lilac and roses that once flanked a doorway now twist and tangle in exuberant abandon, concealing all that lies beneath. But yet we know what's there.

ON DUCK

I see a glimpse of Duck Island in a photograph of a boy on a bicycle. "On Duck," a scribbled label far down on the right corner of the image reads. I imagine someone arranging family pictures in a hurry, perhaps with a stack yet to go through. It's an old photograph, sepia gray. Even in the e-mail version I have just been sent, I can see the tatters around its edges.

The boy on the bicycle seems to have been interrupted; he's seated on the old fenderless bike, one high-topped sneaker type shoe on the ground, his face only partially visible. The face, what I can see of it, is quizzical, perhaps even a bit cheeky; it hints at some secret awareness.

"Hey, I want to take your picture," someone with a camera may have called out.

The boy would have stopped and turned.

"Ok, take my picture," he may have said. "But I have places to go, other things to do."

On Duck Island, however, he couldn't have gone far and he couldn't have gone fast. The ground is marshy: to the right of the boy in the photo are the "boardwalks," constructed wooden walkways–not called, like those in Venice at flood tide, "duckboards"–requisite to easy movement across an uneven, soggy area. This place, now the nesting habitat of the largest colony of Leach's storm petrels in the eastern United States, could not have been made for easy bicycle riding. And how far could the boy have ridden on a 220-acre Maine island off the south coast of Mount Desert Island. "We walked to the other side of the island, where a boat dropped off our supplies," the boy would explain to a reporter many years later; "and we brought everything back to our house in a wheelbarrow." Christmas was the only exception, he said: an airplane flew over and dropped a box containing a turkey, tobacco, and candy.

The boy's father is the lighthouse keeper, and the family lives in the tall angular house that rises up in the background of the photograph. That's a Maine house for sure, an island house. Slightly to the right the wall of a large shed or barn is just visible. The boy has been stopped on ground between the house and the lighthouse. But the white lighthouse, built in 1890, would have been behind the camera and is not visible to us. Neither does this photograph tell us that the ocean pounds in on granite berm only yards away. We cannot hear the ocean that must have drummed continually in the ear of the boy on the bicycle: the boy who lived on Duck.

"We'd love to go out to Duck," we used to say to Lyford Stanley. Lyford, who ran the boat that took us out to our house on Gotts Island, several miles to the west of Duck, never really responded. We knew he had lots to do in the summer, hauling people, freight, and baggage between Bass Harbor and Gotts in the Stanley 36, one of a series of classic Maine boats that he had designed and helped build. And all this was in addition to fishing. We knew there was no harbor or dock at Duck, and the area in the photograph had become a preserve for ornithological research run by the College of the Atlantic in Bar Harbor. Visitors not formally connected with COA were not welcome in the nesting period, April through October. We didn't–couldn't–push the matter. It wouldn't have made any difference if we had. It was clear that Lyford didn't really want to make any special trips out to Duck.

Lyford had left Duck Island behind him years before. He was the boy on the bicycle.

The photograph of Lyford was taken at the far southern point of Duck. I have another image of the island–in fact, several, if I count the various maps displayed on the College of the Atlantic website. Great Duck (there is also a small one) is shaped like a stretched out parenthesis or kidney bean, "elongated north-south with a long axis of 1.9 km and a short (east-west) axis of .7 km," according to the informative description provided by the COA. Most of Duck Island is a joint tenancy of the State of Maine and the Maine Nature Conservancy. Its perimeter is a rocky belt that slopes gently to sea level on the southwest end of the island and rises in "sheer cliffs approximately 10m in height at points along the eastern and northern shores." A low-lying brackish wetland at the narrow "waist" of the island, occupies what the scientists call an "old surge canal" that once separated the island into two parts, north and south. This area has been dubbed "The Slough of Despond" on the COA map. The name, recalling John Bunyan's *Pilgrim's Progress* and the place where the Christian pilgrim becomes mired in sin and despair, is, I learn, of more mundane origin: "I called it the Slough of Despond after a particularly hot & bothersome day counting gulls, and the name has stuck," COA's chief ornithologist John Anderson explained in a message responding to my query.

But there is much that any map or graphic description leaves out. Partial or isolated views of an island do not explain its presence and pattern. The "segregation of parts is independent of knowledge and meaning," psychologist Wolfgang Kohler wrote in his classic 1947 work on gestalt cognition. "Darkness and mist," obscure the element, whether temporal or spatial, that is "segregated" from the whole. Whatever clarity, or understanding, we can achieve must come from putting the pieces together. On Duck Island, a space that appears demarcated from its surrounding sea, a limited but real cast of characters have made their entrances and their exits. They came, and went, for different reasons; but the boy on the bicycle, the islanders who preceded him, and those who arrived later–some seeking, like Bunyan's Christian hero, help for pain and despair–are all linked in the history of Duck Island.

Charles McLane tells us in his masterful history, *Islands of the Mid-Maine Coast*, that Great Duck was named as early as 1720, was inhabited first by members of the Gilley family from Baker's Island, and became, in the late 1850's, the home of Charles and Mary Harding, who had recently arrived from Stoke Poges in the British Cotswolds.

The Hardings settled on the north side of the island, acquired title to the entire island in 1867, and by 1882, through brute hard work, had become reasonably comfortable: they owned about 200 sheep, and according to local newspaper report, 60-100 lambs were sold each fall. But life was soon to change for the Hardings and the nephew who lived with them. Stove embers from the chimney are said to have ignited the newly tarred roof of their house, which, along with adjacent outbuildings, was destroyed in the resulting fire. The family decamped for Gotts Island and after spending several years living in a fish house by the shore, purchased the substantial house on the west side of Gotts which remained in the family through World War II.

North of the Slough of Despond, within easy walking distance of the spot where young Lyford Stanley posed with his bicycle and close to the land where the Hardings had been settled, another image imposes itself. A man wearing a French beret crouches down to feed a small pig. A pony looks on attentively, and the curved roof of a yurt dominates the background space. The ground is spare and rocky; only a few skinny spruce rise up behind the yurt. The man is a psychiatrist and gestalt practitioner named Dr. George Cloutier. He is slim and bearded, appearing older than his forty-four years. He looks directly at the camera. He and the place where the photograph is taken are the subject of a short essay in the "On Scene" section of *Newsweek's* July 21, 1975, issue; the piece is titled "Gestalt on the Rocks."

George Cloutier was an adventurer. He had spent time at a weather station at Thule, Greenland; delivered a baby in the back of a single-engine plane near fort Yukon, Alaska; led an eight-man expedition up Mount McKinley. And he was, apparently, a man who loved islands. "My life here on Duck is more meaningful, useful, content," he told a writer for *Down East* Magazine in 1975. He had "kicked" his big city life as a successful psychiatrist; he had become a "happy man." Cloutier sees his private patients in Bangor on Fridays, *Down East* tells us; then he flies in his own small plane back to Duck Island (to the runway he built himself) and to patients he treats as full-time residents on the island. When the plastic dome he built on the island did not work out, he built another dwelling. He uses a well dug over a hundred years ago, perhaps a remnant of the Hardings' tenancy on the island. Dr. Cloutier calls gestalt therapy "one of the newest humanistic trends in mental health treatment." "We teach people self-utilization: how to relate better to others, and how to take and accept life's risks," he says; "I feel that most people utilize only ten to fifteen percent of their potential." In the *Newsweek* article he is more expansive: on an island, he says, "people cut loose and have a chance to be themselves."

In 1975, we had been for eleven years summer residents of Gotts Island, where we were far less prone to "cutting loose." Our perception of Duck Island was vague at best, a tissue of rumor and myth. If the local fisherman knew more about the island, they didn't talk much about it to summer islanders like us. Duck, a distant speck of land, its lighthouse just barely visible, was particularly other. If all other islands remain something of a mystery to the inhabitants of small islands, this island, defined in the imagination as the home of bizarre people, was all the more so. Any person encountered on the dock at Bass Harbor who looked remotely strange might be thought of as destined for the essentially unknown and far less understood Duck Island. "Going out to Duck, huh?" a teen-aged neighbor once asked friends of ours who, though wearing odd floppy sun hats and layers of white sun cream on their faces, were simply waiting for a boat that would take them to Gotts Island. The teen-ager, like most of us, couldn't fit Dr. Cloutier's community into any pattern that she knew.

Yet Cloutier's Duck Island was hardly a unique experiment and its language of "self utilization," of the need to realize one's personal potential, was emblematic of its time. In California, at the Esalen community founded at Big Sur in the early 60s, people were also "cutting loose," and gestalt therapy, the attempt to "focus on the subject's conscious experience and construction of the here-and-now," came into its own. George Cloutier studied gestalt therapeutic methods in California in 1971 and 1972 with James Simkin, a well-known second-generation therapist who worked with the more famous master, Frederick (Fritz) Perls, at Esalen in the late 1960s. Simkin emphasized the interaction of the individual with the total environment when he argued in his book, *Mini-Lectures in Gestalt Therapy*, that "unaware behavior is the result not of the unconscious or preconscious, but rather, of the organism's not being in touch with its external environment: unmet needs influence our sensory involvement with the world."

Boston psychotherapist Richard Borofsky told me that he could readily understand George Cloutier's attraction to the environment of Duck Island: why he gave up, as the *Newsweek* article says, a flourishing psychiatric practice in Boston, a closet full of Brooks Brothers suits, a Porsche, and lunches at the Harvard Club. Dr. Borofsky, who knew Cloutier professionally, had visited the Duck Island Community but was never a practitioner there. He is, however, also a lover of islands, and of Duck Island in particular. He owns land that once belonged to the Harding family, passed through other owners, and then became part of the site of Cloutier's experimental colony. This is now the only private piece of property on Duck, a plot of about five acres where Borofsky and his wife have built a substantial house and spend several weeks each summer. On the day I spoke with him, he was just back from a trip to California: to Esalen.

From Rich Borofsky I learned that George Cloutier started out as a summer resident on Duck and then turned a personal retreat into a "life work." And it must have been difficult work. Although the Duck Island community offered short-term therapy for more common life problems such as marital stress, some of the half dozen or so people in longer-term residence suffered serious mental illness. The *Newsweek* account provided some cases in point: "Martha, a manic depressive who ran away from a state hospital where she had been administered heavy doses of tranquilizing drugs; Susan, a brilliant marine biologist who wears a tattered parka and a wounded stare; Sylvia, a Maine bank teller whose jaw muscles are knotted and whose teeth enamel is worn off because, Cloutier says, 'she kept her mouth clamped shut for years against the rage she felt': and Jack, a witty, formerly alcoholic Episcopal priest who has lost his parish." "One of the women killed a sheep with a knife," Rich Borofsky reported to me. The unfortunate sheep would have been part of the animal entourage that included, in addition to the pig and the pony, a pet doe, a 200-pound Newfoundland dog named Melissa, two cats and a beagle.

The patients paid $450 a month, surely not a lot for room, board, and treatment (rental of a house on Gotts Island, with an uncertain amount of running water and no heat or electricity would have been about $200 per month at that time). They participated, Dr. Borofsky explained, in a process of "expressive therapy" aimed at emotional release. Sometimes, he said, the patients were joined by the Coast Guardsmen who were at that time still staffing the lighthouse; given the isolation of their job, they were apparently desperate enough to seek human company at Cloutier's sessions.

But it was always the identification of Duck as an island, a space traditionally (if often erroneously) equated with limits and differentiation, that, in Cloutier's terms, "made the enormous difference" in his work. Concentrating, even distilling, experience, the island enabled that "immediacy of sensory involvement" sought by psychologist Simkin. As it had been for Robinson Crusoe, that early fictive island dweller who perhaps also "actualized himself" in years of lonely insular exile, the island as therapeutic space is the place of the "here and now"

Still, an island–whether pastoral ideal, therapeutic site, or a combination of the two–is ultimately not enough. The "successful" therapy, psychologist Ernest Becker argued in a lecture published in *The Gestalt Journal* in 1993, turns out a person "who has come to see the conditions of life on this planet as they really are." This individual no longer needs the island as a space for self-actualization. Like Lyford Stanley, he or she can leave the island behind and take on the "conditions of life" offered in the broader world.

In different epochs of the past, all the inhabitants of Duck departed for destinations and lives I cannot know. But I suspect they did not see themselves as turned out of Eden. Lyford Stanley left to attend school on the mainland, and his father left his lighthouse post when new staff were hired, and, ultimately, the Coast Guard took over the lightkeeping responsibilities. The Hardings, as we have seen, were driven out by the fire, but though living on Gotts, continued, with another island family, to pasture a flock of about 140 sheep on Duck right up until the beginning of World War II. At that point the two families sold the island together but still continued, throughout the war, to care for the sheep of the new owner. None of the fragments I have of the story of George Cloutier's community exactly explain its demise. Rich Borofsky reported that he does not know the details of the last chapters of Cloutier's life but he told me of a marker erected on Duck in Cloutier's memory. It's near the old airstrip and the Slough of Despond and dedicated to a man who loved islands.

The birds did not leave Duck Island. And, as the College of the Atlantic website so well documents, the island as laboratory and nature preserve remains. The guillemots, burrowed down into their small rocky strongholds, are but one species comprising a vast population of seabirds occupying the Maine offshore islands: a number equal to half of all seabirds east of the Mississippi. As early as 1900, Duck's seabird population was protected; the first lighthouse keeper was also the warden. A visitor to the island in 1913 reported large numbers of dead trees and gulls nesting in among the broken stumps. The gulls are presumed to have killed the trees, perhaps nesting there in order to escape domestic animals brought on by the light-keepers. Under the large boulders in the berm that marks the island's periphery, the black guillemots build their nests, "laying one to three eggs, which they incubate in crevices along the shoreline." The research team from the College tries to band the guillemot chicks, but the rocky substrate of the nesting and roosting habitat quickly wears out the bands.

At the same time, some 5000 pairs of storm petrels forage as far as 200 miles offshore and return after dark to the breeding colony. They nest in shallow burrows up to 1 meter in length and lay a single egg. Their name, "petrel," derives from St. Peter, who is said to have walked on water; but the COA ornithologists say that "strictly speaking, the petrels don't 'walk' on water, but dabble their feet while fluttering over the surface." Not far away, in the Slough of Despond, migratory black ducks–for whom the island is named–stop off for a rest every autumn, while the much more numerous eiders build warm and insulated nests on neighboring Little Duck. This smaller Duck, unlike the larger, has never known permanent human habitation.

On a brilliant day in August 2005 my husband and I did make it out to Duck. We were invited to join an expedition of schoolteachers participating in an environmental workshop at the College of the Atlantic. The COA launch picked us up at Gotts Island. Scott Swann, a COA instructor and our Gotts neighbor, was the guide.

The trip to Duck felt like an adventure, a long anticipated event finally coming true. Off the eastern edge of the island, as the boat rocked on its mooring, we piled, three by three, into the dinghy that landed us on the island's rocky belt: the only way to arrive on an island with no real harbor or dock. Once the passengers were all offloaded, the dinghy was hauled up on a pulley into a boathouse at the top of the high rocks.

We walked the path toward the southern shore, to the lighthouse, and the very place where the unknown photographer had caught the young Lyford Stanley on film. We stood on the "boardwalks." We listened attentively as the ornithologists discussed their project on Duck; we saw the petrel chicks and the guillemot nests, our eyes squinting in the bright sunlight that reflected off the pure white lighthouse.

The path in the other direction, to the northern side of the island, was mainly shady. Weeds and brush clot what remains of George Cloutier's landing strip; and while his community's large log eating hall is still there, assorted small cabins and the yurts have all but disappeared. Duck is of course not entirely uninhabited–the ornithologists are regularly there–but the appearance of desertion is everywhere, the remains of the island's various periods of habitation seemingly flowing into one another. A few foundation markers hark back to the time preceding Cloutier's construction. A straggling stone wall, meandering down toward the shore, may have been built by the Hardings, or possibly even the family that preceded them. Rock and stone endure beyond neglected wood and frame.

And then, too soon, our visit to Duck was ending. The dinghy was lowered from its high perch back into the water. Again three by three, we clambered awkwardly aboard, and then, with even more difficulty, climbed from the dinghy into the still rocking COA launch. Especially for the uninitiated, neither arrival nor leave-taking at Duck Island is easy, but finally, with the boarding accomplished, we were all settled in the boat. The engine moved into action, and we began our route home.

We had gone, we had seen; but once back on Gotts, our accustomed place, everything slipped back. We were seeing what we had always seen from the easternmost side of "our" island. The lighthouse, the paths, the remains of Dr. Cloutier's community fell into a pattern of their own, strangely still opaque and distant. Like all the islands we see from our own speck of land, the Ducks, big and little, may beckon but still retain their remoteness. Island to island connections are undeniable but nonetheless remain always tenuous. The open fields that marked the old Cloutier property, the ground we had walked, were now a vague green emptiness, like the background of a canvas awaiting the image. The lighthouse that had blinded us with its white presence on the day we visited was once again just barely visible from the granite on Gotts' eastern edge, a mere outline.

This was the image we knew. We organize and interpret–imagine and remember–Duck Island as best we can. Lyford Stanley's daughter could not tell me exactly why her father left Duck Island or why he did not want to speak about that departure: "He was an energetic man, and he never would have been happy on a small island," she said. Neither could she could throw any light on why her father was unwilling to return to Duck, even briefly. I think we must be content with that, and learn what we can from a photo of a man with a pig and a pony, or one of a boy on a bicycle on a small island, a boy who went on to live an active, productive, and essentially mainland-based life and died at age 81, not on a small island, but in a hospital in Bangor.

DIAMONDS

On the afternoon of July 21, 1960, having eaten lunch at a diner in Belfast, Maine, Mrs. Strauss arrived at the island wearing –if we believe the waitress who served her at the diner– "lots of diamond rings."

The next morning, July 22, 1960, Thorstein Larsen, a retired engineering professor and, like Mrs. Strauss, a summer resident of the island, recorded in his diary: "Strauss cottage burned during the night and Mrs. Strauss burned to death." Thirty-three years later, in 1993, another island resident, Rita Johnson Kenway, in a book titled *Gotts Island Maine: Its People 1880-1992*, described the narrow escape of Mr. Strauss, the housekeeper, and a visiting child. As for Mrs. Strauss, Rita noted that the coroner had sifted through the ashes and found only "tiny charred pieces of bone."

There is no mention of diamonds. But that's not surprising. Diamonds are an anomaly in a place where old clothes are kept on rusted hooks winter after winter; where in the 1990's a Smith College graduate still wore a jacket she had purchased as a student in Northampton in 1937; where, inexplicably, a leather jacket once worn by a World War II pilot hangs, as if waiting to be worn once again, from a beam in my barn.

The diamonds don't belong to our ordinary island lives; they are part of the ever ambiguous and elusive quality of a place that keeps its own secrets, floating, as Maine poet Ruth Moore once wrote, "in its own sea." Although Mrs. Strauss' stepson was married to my older sister and I have spent forty summers on the island, the reported diamonds are as mysterious to me as the coastal fog that locks us into gauzy cocoons, the mute fragments of lives left behind when a year-round community founded in the eighteenth century disappeared, and the empty summer houses that wait through the long winter, bearing up to the forces of wind, storm, and grumbling rocks that hold at bay an angry sea. Once I have returned to another coast and another life each September, the diamonds illumine a place that defies mere physical detail; rather, like a fantasy island that emerges as a trick of atmospheric conditions, it "looms" in the imagination.

But back on the island each summer, imagination meets geography once again. I know with my feet the trails that I walk or jog each morning, the wooded track that bisects the island from west to east, and the meandering path by the sea that takes me through the old Strauss property. I know where the way is broad or narrow, the places where the sea comes fully into view beyond the spruce and slabs of granite, the spots where spongy earth gives way to rocky outcropping. And in memory I know the old Strauss cottage, a house I visited at age ten when I came up to the island to visit my sister and her then young family. A deeply felt physical landscape empowers that memory: the child's fear of a darkened room whose wall was a shallow cliff, the massive stone fireplace dominating the main space where, it is thought, Mrs. Strauss met her death ten years later. I imagine flames leaping up toward the upper gallery that provided access to the various bedrooms, one of which I myself must have slept in.

After the fire that he had so narrowly escaped and the horrific death of his wife, Mr. Strauss never returned to the Island. Several years later, his daughter Bella, a fiercely independent and feisty physician, built a new house at the very edge of the granite rocks by the sea, some yards from the site of the original structure. In the usual way of things, trees and brush grew up where the old house had been. Presumably too, Bella had the remains of the old house bulldozed over. At any rate, in all the years that I have been going to the island as an adult, I have never seen a single trace of that house. This is an oddity in a place where old granite foundations, stony footprints of structures long since disappeared, tend to remain: strange markers encountered in places where a century of relentless spruce growth has transformed a once open field into a dark forest.

The diamonds–if we give any credibility to the story told by the Belfast waitress–would have disappeared along with everything else, sinking, like memory itself, ever more deeply into soft mossy ground. The large outlines of the tale of the fire remain, even duly recorded; the details, so open to imaginative, even surprising or shocking, construction, elude.

But perhaps, as Barbara Hurd observes in *Walking the Wrack Line,* the details don't really matter. It's "what happens next" that counts: another story. Years later, in her account of Mrs. Strauss' death, my sister, no longer married to Mrs. Strauss' stepson, told me with apparent seriousness that "only the heart remained, sort of like Joan of Arc or the saints; and Bella dumped the heart in the trash bin at the IGA store in Southwest Harbor. You know Bella, no sentiment there."

A heart? I'm thinking about the tiny bone fragments that Rita Kenway mentioned in her book. What, exactly, did "happen next"? More important, does it matter that stories conflict with one another? In tales of loss, we can always fill in the gaps with more detail, more stories. The process goes on even when the old tellers and the old actors are long gone: Rita, the island's self-appointed historian, had sadly lost her memory to dementia well before her death several years ago; Bella, the Strauss daughter, died some half dozen years ago (having told me one sunny July morning toward the end of her life that if I ever found her "toes up in the kitchen," I was to call the proper authorities and make sure that Molly, her Irish water spaniel, was well taken care of). Since Bella actually died at her winter home in New Hampshire, I never learned what happened to Molly.

"And then there was that psychic she was involved with in the 1940's," my sister said. We were discussing why, unlike the others living there, Mrs. Strauss did not get out of the burning house in time. Here was yet another thread. My sister was referring to Edgar Cayce, who, according to Wikipedia, "claimed the ability to channel answers to questions on subjects such as health or Atlantis while in a self-induced trance." My sister said she had seen a transcript of a session with Cayce or one of his disciples. Asked how she felt about fire, Mrs. Strauss had reportedly responded: "It fascinates me. It makes me powerless to move."

If the story of the psychic grows murky at this point, the tone of Thorstein Larsen's diary account of the Strauss fire, the voice of the engineer, serves as corrective. "Luckily," Thorstein recorded in his diary the morning after the Strauss fire, "it was a calm night, or the whole island might have gone." Here is a stark reality. Gotts, like so many other island communities, had known only too well the fierce power of fire. Even now, issues of fire preparedness, of the inadequacy of the Indian tanks provided by the township on the mainland–there is no way that I, for example, could ever heft an Indian tank full of water–dominate neighborly discussions. We know the old stories: the tale of the Methodist church that reportedly burned to the ground when the desperate next-door neighbor set his house alight in order to collect the insurance money, and matters got out of hand; the spiteful islander who is said to have burned down his neighbor's barn in a fit of pique, causing the unfortunate neighbor to leave the island permanently. And we all know about the most famous fire of all, the story of the Peterson cottage that mysteriously burned to the ground on a wintry night in 1926, just when the island's year-round population was struggling to forestall the collective death that was to come in 1930.

None of the islanders living within a mile of that fire claimed any knowledge of the death of Elizabeth Peterson, the well-off woman "from away" who had chosen to live year round on the island. The ruined remains of Miss Peterson's house were discovered by island fishermen only the next day when their boat took them past the site. As for Miss Peterson, it was simply assumed–as it was in the case of Mrs. Strauss– that she had died through a mishap with a kerosene lamp. Only the stone foundation of the Peterson house now remains, silent evidence of an event that we cannot really explain.

In 1960, the year of the Strauss fire, Miss Peterson's death still stood large in island memory and lore. The missing details were simply integrated into both the story and the place it embraces and creates. "No place is a place," Wallace Stegner has written, "until things that have happened to it are remembered in history, ballads, [and] legends." We live as much in the stories–"legends"–of a place as in the place itself.

I didn't live on the island in the summer of 1960. I did not witness the Strauss fire. I know only what I read or am told, trusting a reporter like Thorstein Larsen, who is so precise in his description of the facts: "Most of the people on the island got over there," he wrote, "and they stayed until 4:15 a.m. [when] the Coast Guard arrived and was ready to douse the fire." Thorstein meant the other summer families, who, like himself, had replaced the old year-round island community that had been gone for thirty years. Some of them were the descendants or the early "rusticators" who traveled from Boston, New York, and Philadelphia to summer first on the mainland, and later on the offshore islands, of Maine. Beginning in the 1930's and 40's, and sometimes earlier, these families took over the few remaining village houses and, in some cases, erected new ones.

Thorstein Larsen has been dead for years, his wife and daughter Inger also gone; but a few senior members of neighboring families remain–the families who live across the field, down the hill, or along the path to the meadow on the northernmost shore. They are the witnesses. "Inger ran over to my house and told me to get the children out of bed and go down to the shore," one told me. Inger, as recounted in Rita Kenway's book, had heard the old Strauss truck, the "blue rocket," "bumpity-bumping" over the roots and ruts of the track in front of the Larsen house; she had heard the driver (probably the maid who had managed to escape the blazing house) shouting out the alarm: "Fire!"

No one remembered who it was who rang the warning bell by the shore. This was the same bell that had once called worshippers to services at the ill-fated Methodist church. When the church burned down, old Montell Gott, the last Gott–in fact the last person–to live all year round on the island, a man not given to destroying anything useful, reportedly moved the surviving bell to its present spot by the dock to be sounded in the event of disaster. The women and children, along with the elderly Miss Caroline Holmes and her teen-aged niece Virginia, "huddled together" by the shore, close to the bell, Rita Kenway wrote; they talked about "how they would go into the water if the flames threatened." Left in his paddock, Virginia Holmes' frenzied horse ran back and forth as flames lit up the dark night sky.

I was not there to hear the bell that night, have never heard it. For me, it is simply a presence, quietly keeping watch in its place just to the left of the dock. It marks a gathering point for island arrivals, the spot where we pile up the bags and supplies that we have hauled out from the mainland and now must transport–for my family by wheelbarrow–up to the house.

As Mrs. Strauss climbed out of a local lobster boat and stepped on to the shore of the island that July day in 1960, whatever baggage she brought along would have been assembled by the bell. From there it would have gone out to the Strauss cottage in the "blue rocket": the same vehicle that Inger Larsen would hear much later that night coming along the rutted path, the same that now, years later, molders in rusted fragments in the woods beyond our back field.

When I visited the island three years after Mrs. Strauss' death, now with a husband and an infant son, the catastrophe at the Strauss cottage was not mentioned. Perhaps it was still too recent, the pain and shock still felt. It was yet to be determined "what happens next," how the event, like that of the much earlier Peterson fire, would be woven into an island narrative.

For island stories, like the geography of which they are a part, are the work of time and distance. It doesn't really matter that the story my sister told me may have been pure fabrication, that no body parts survived, no diamonds lost. The vital life of a place depends on the slow accretion of detail, remembered, refigured, and in some way recounted. That's what the island is. Its landscape is a malleable field that both forms, and is formed by, the work of the imagination. A tragic event on a July night can turn readily into a gothic tale. Conflicting modes of seeing, knowing, and telling come into play here. Nothing is smooth or clearly defined.

In the summer of 2009, Hurricane Bill swept through the Gulf of Maine and produced a sea that most of us on the island had never witnessed over decades of summers.

Refusing containment by the island's granite margins, giant waves swept over the rocks and into the land, washing around (though not destroying) the house that Bella had built and boiling furiously up into the ground where the original Strauss house once stood. I watched the edges, the protecting, or defining, borders of the island disappear in the watery onslaught. The categories and forms we thought we knew—"land," "sea," "edge"—all fell into confusion, the diamonds, if they were ever there, carried off into that raging sea.

4

CROSSINGS

*"And may there be no moaning of the bar,
When I put out to sea"*

ALFRED LORD TENNYSON,
"CROSSING THE BAR"

I'm looking at a photograph of myself crossing a bar that at low tide links two sibling islands but at high water becomes one with the sea. I am one element in a land (sea) scape, a minimal part to be sure, but one acutely aware of the ongoing motion of the ocean currents. I am not, like Tennyson's narrator, "putting out to sea." I'm just on my way to visit a friend on a neighboring island. I am moving swiftly and purposefully toward my destination.

But some crossings and arrivals are unintended. Such was the case when the bodies of two unknown men drowned at sea, washed up on the shore of a small island, and were taken to join, in their very anonymity, the order of the local cemetery: the same place where, in a twenty-first century island funeral more than a hundred years later, a bevy of kites would float jubilantly, like a moving cloud, above a simple ritual of burial. This is also the cemetery where my son, remembered in a childhood incident carrying a pair of stringed marionettes (once called "motions") is buried, the motion of his life extinguished.

In a small village cemetery in northern Spain, I remember on an above-ground grave the collaged photograph of a man leading cows from one field to another. The man had died young. In the photograph he is still a living and moving presence. He is engaged in a literal crossing, though one that now suggests a continuation from life into death.

We do not put photographs on gravestones in our small Maine island cemetery, that is not our way; but yet, the dead interred within the fence marking the cemetery's boundaries also exert a presence. And the cemetery itself is a kind of island. When the old rotted fence was removed to make way for a new one, the place itself, and the gravestones within it, seemed dramatically changed, its islandness denied. Only when the new fence was completed, was form conferred once again on the village of the dead. Form, poet Mary Oliver has written, is "certainty"; it "strikes a note in the universe unlike any other." And, I would add, form reinforces memory by providing a site where it may be sustained. It gives us a sense of the "in" and the "out," and even more important, it enables movement between the two.

CROSSING THE BAR

Despite the unevenness of the land beneath my feet, I walk as fast as I can because I must keep track of the time, visit my friend on Little Gotts, and make sure to return before the surface I'm now walking on shrinks to a thread, ultimately to disappear. Then the ocean takes over again. It will separate the two related islands, but open the way to arriving, or departing, boats. One connection is broken, but another, this with the mainland or other islands, affirmed. Linkages change. They come and they go; their fundamental character is motion.

I have already walked the higher, stony part of the bar that remains always above the tide. I have passed the place where the gray-white bones of a dead seagull lie withering at the wrack line of dried seaweed, where the skiffs of the island families sit upended on the beach, and a scattering of motorboats sit dumbly in the adjacent water. Boats spend a lot of time waiting. In use, there is a quick rush of sound and energy, and then, the trip or errand completed, they once again rest silent.

In walking this surface that is both barrier and connection I feel the estrangement of one who moves over a margin. Perhaps no one can be at home in a place where all is in flux, where keeping track of the ever-changing tide is essential. Is this a place at all; or is it, rather, a transitory site of experience, whether imagined or remembered? No, I am not "at home" here on this bar; I need to keep moving toward the small island that beckons ahead.

The bar is defined by motion. Whether walking on its surface when the tide is out or moving over it in a boat at high water, we are always crossing to some destination, some inconsequential, others laden with meaning, even if not recognized at the time. And it's the not-recognized that can become the most important, the event or circumstance later to be re-lived with renewed significance. That's why I remember so clearly the day, so many years ago, when Lyford Stanley's boat went aground when attempting to cross over the bar.

It must have been just about at the point I am now crossing. The tide was coming but still a barrier to a boat leaving Gotts Island for Bass Harbor, our mainland port. It was late summer and we were embarked on our final departure of the season. A miserable day with the rain pouring down. But it wasn't the weather that was unusual. It was the fact that Lyford, who knew these waters so well, misjudged the water level on the bar. We had been passengers on this boat so many times, and never had Lyford made the error of running aground in low water.

With the tide coming, the waters gradually rising, the halt had been temporary of course. Surely this was not a major incident. Yet, I have never forgotten it. I remember the aggressive churning of the incoming tidal water as it advanced to take over the domain it claimed as its own but had not yet conquered. In the boat, we were momentarily caught in two zones, land and sea; and in two times, low and high tide. This was not Tennyson's "Crossing the Bar" where the sea, at a full high tide, is dominant, "too full for sound and foam." The bar may indicate a line between life and death in Tennyson's poem, but it remains, unlike the physical barrier we ultimately crossed over that day, a metaphor after all.

It will only be a matter of minutes until we can pass over, Lyford had said. Then we were on our way again, all too soon arriving at the dock in Bass Harbor to begin the task of unloading the bags and baggage. We were enacting the repeated end of summer ritual of departure. It always culminated with the final shout, "We'll see you next year." This year was no exception: our voices floated out over the harbor as Lyford turned the boat to return to the island.

Yes, this must be the spot where we had to wait for the rising water on that day years ago. I see once again that churning tide, feel in memory the cold pelting rain. Huddled together, we were wet and chilled, concerned that our bags and gear stay dry, eager to be in transit again. And we hadn't noticed the most essential fact. That's the inexcusable thing: we hadn't seen that something else was seriously wrong. Having put aside Lyford's quiet references over the summer that he felt less strong than usual, we didn't know on that stormy day that a serious illness, privately suppressed for months, was now completing its drastic course. Two months later a phone call from Maine would inform us that Lyford had died in the hospital in Bangor. There was to be no next year.

With the tide still well out and my visit to Little Gotts accomplished, I am almost back to Big Gotts and my own home. I have reached the higher ground where the carcass of the sea bird whitens in the sun in its crusty bed of seaweed, and the boats moored nearby, gently acknowledging the movement of the tide, still wait. Yes, I'm imagining, with the tide almost all the way in, Lyford would have easily crossed over the bar on his return trip to the island that rainy, late summer day. There would have been no delays. On a tide now "too full for sound and foam," it would have been an unremarkable crossing.

STRINGS

They were known in the seventeenth century as "motions." We know them as puppets.

We also know them as Hansel, Gretel, Zimzazabim, Rauber, and Teufel; and they live with their fellow puppets in a green bag in a drawer under the eaves in our Gotts Island house. The original group, joined gradually over the years by others, have been resident there for more than five decades. Some of the stitching has come loose on Gretel's dress. Hansel's hat sits at a lopsided angle. The puffy gray beard on the sea captain is frayed, and the spring that operates the mouth of the crocodile has lost its snap. But generally, everything remains. Change comes slowly on the island.

We produced our first puppet show at Gotts Island in the summer of 1966. We did not have the theatre then. We used the wide, double-door frame between the front hall and the living room as a stage, and the children sat on straw matting on the floor. It was an imaginary stage; the young audience had to pretend they didn't see John and me acting the parts in the show. A visiting two year old howled with terror as the little figures "spoke" to their audience. "It's only make believe," her mother, who was writing a dissertation on Renaissance drama, told her.

By 1968 we had the theatre. John made it out of leftover fake-wood paneling we had bought for the boys' bedroom.

It was cheap and bent easily, but it did the job. John decorated the theatre with abstract pine trees, waves—and, marking the historical moment, a large peace sign. The curtain was made from the green fabric that our neighbor Rita Kenway had used for her downstairs bedroom windows. Once completed, the new theater could be set up between the big rolling doors of the barn, while the audience gathered in the yard. As in Shakespeare's original Globe Theatre, good weather was a definite plus.

I recall nothing of the plot of that original puppet performance in 1966; nor do I remember in detail any of our plots over the years. Usually put together quickly, jotted down on an old yellow pad, our stories were at best mundane variations on the triumph of innocence over experience, good over evil. There was no ambiguity; everyone, young and old, knew that a happy ending was assured. If "highbrow classical stories" transformed into vernacular texts proved extremely popular at puppet shows in seventeenth-century England–I cite Victoria Nelson's book, *Secret Life of Puppets*–our plots were simply "vernacular," or more exactly narrowly local, in the sense that they usually derived from some aspect of island experience in a given summer. It was always the same cast of characters: the handsome young man, fair maiden, bad devil, nasty ne'er-do-well, magician (also very important for plots), and a crocodile that could represent all the animal forces, negative or positive, of nature. Sometimes the red, gaping-mouthed Crocodile became the henchman of Rauber, threatening the good

Hansel, Gretel, and old sea captain; more often, crocodile was the friendly deputy of the good hero, swallowing up evil, dragging it down to a watery grave.

Our "motions" were part of us. We liked to think of them as family, sharing in our lives but with an independence of their own. When, decades after our original purchase of the puppets, we added Foxie as a new member of the troupe–a little fox with brilliant eyes, a bright green coat and jaunty expression, created in the same toy factory in Germany where the others were born–John and I wrote a story about the puppets, with Foxie as the main character.

The occasion was our granddaughter Astrid's fourth birthday; we were celebrating not only a new and instantly loved puppet, but a new generation of children. We called the book *Foxie's First Winter*. We imagined the appealing little puppet living a life with his companions in winter after all the human inhabitants had departed from the island. The plot, simple enough, was a homely reminder of Heidigger's suggestion that "objects truly flourish only in that midnight reality that shields them from our view." Foxie and his companions definitely flourish. With excited motion, they jump out of their drawer, exult in the departure of the human denizens of the house–us–and engage enthusiastically in a feast with the resident elves (yes, elves habitually live on small Maine islands). Though not quite a place "where the wild things are," the island is transformed into the domain of small felt creatures with bright heads and faces, empty bodies, and German names. They move by their own agency and they know where they are going, confident that there will be always be another winter and then another summer.

Puppets requiring strings just wouldn't have been right for our story. In fact, strings, which the "motion men" used to give movement to those seventeenth-century puppets, did not work for us at all. For us latecomer, amateur "motion people," string puppets would have demanded far more skill and dexterity than we could muster. That's a major reason why the two rather beautiful string marionettes that we had received as a gift remained interlopers and never joined the group in the green bag.

But their story is more complicated than that. It's also a story of a small, six-year old boy who lived on an island and went off one summer morning to visit his aunt, who was living that summer in a house reachable only by a path through the woods. The mosquitoes were bad that summer, especially in the woods. The boy's aunt, his mother's sister, gave him two lovely marionettes that she had purchased in Mexico the preceding winter. Not remembering the mosquitoes, his aunt warned him to be careful not to tangle the strings on the walk back to his own house. So the boy–it was my son, Ben, this male and modern red riding hood–set out on his way through the woods, across the Parker family's field, and up the hill toward home. He wanted to obey instructions, to hold the marionettes aloft and keep the long strings taut. But he was just not tall enough. He was forced to keep his arms raised as high as possible, leaving no hand free to deal with the ravenous mosquitoes.

I was out on the front deck of our house when I saw him emerge from the woods into Harriet Parker's field. I noticed his odd posture, his awkward walk. I could see that he was carrying something but it was not clear what it was. It was only as he started up the path and approached our house that I saw, first the marionettes and second, the mosquitoes that swirled hungrily and mercilessly around him. By this time, still holding the strings taut, he was crying in misery, his pain, despite his bumping walk, transmitting nothing to the brightly colored marionettes.

Running down the path to help him, then throwing the stringed creatures aside, I could only hug my son close and commend him for heroic service. Brief though it was, there was agony in that moment, for me as well as for him, a kind of pain that remains, clearly marked in memory. Love, fear, anger, sympathy–all came together in an unexpected, and at the time inexplicable, confusion of emotion. I wept with my son.

As for the boy himself, he probably did not remember the marionette incident in years to come. He had a lot of life yet to live, much grander adventures to experience, distant worlds to see: all this before a plane crash in one of those worlds twenty years later would end it all. I would be thousands of miles away on that day. I would not be able to comfort and praise, not then, not ever. But perhaps I had wept that summer day on the island because I knew that our young Hansels are all vulnerable–to the slings and arrows that we cannot protect them against, to all the forces that are much larger than those encapsulated in nasty mosquitoes, or a robber/ne'er do well and a small red devil with green beady eyes.

As for the marionettes, I still see them, untouched by mere human suffering and lying motionless in a maze of tangled strings.

DECORUM

Ted, our summer neighbor for many years, had died the preceding spring. Now, a small group of us, twenty or so, gathered on a July day in the island cemetery to bury his ashes. Some had come in boats, like those famously pictured in NC Wyeth's painting, "Island Funeral." Some, like myself, were already living on the island. Above us as we stood around the burial site, a half-dozen kites danced toward the sky, their strings firmly anchored to the posts of the cemetery fence.

"Ted always loved to fly kites right here on the hill, where, on a breezy day, the updraft from the shore below kept them aloft."

That was his daughter speaking. Yes, the kites were right. And so was the timing. As if on schedule, the breeze had come up just an hour before we were to gather for the burial. A bevy of bright butterflies, Japanese box kites, homemade old-fashioned kites with long trailing tails–all fluttered high in a luminous sky, climbing, swooping, then rising again, their strings stretching taut

Rob, Ted's grandson, held the box of ashes, one of those simple green cardboard boxes one receives from the crematorium. "No need for a fancy urn," we had been told when we buried our son's ashes in this same cemetery; and Ted had apparently held to this same opinion. He had died two months short of his 100th birthday, but still with enough presence of mind to make his wishes known.

Although he hadn't been physically strong enough to come to the island for a number of years, Ted had remained a community icon, the oldest islander still living. We all felt the loss, the space left by an important missing part. He was one of us.

Rob was placing the box of ashes carefully in the ground. With grace and decorum, his mother spoke movingly of her father and his life as one of the early "summer people" on Gotts Island. He had come with his family as a boy, soon after the First World War. In the early years of their marriage, he and his wife Jane had wintered on the island, burning through many cords of wood, living as almost the sole inhabitants in a time when the yeat-round fishing community had largely departed. He sailed a boat called The Rill, often accompanied by Jolie, his standard white poodle.

All but the youngest members of the group now standing in the cemetery remembered these things. All remembered the man flying kites in the field by the white fence of the cemetery.

But Ted's great granddaughter, aged four, the lone child in attendance, did not. Bored and restless, she was not listening to the remarks the group was now sharing. She had other things on her mind: the family's stone, in place at the gravesite since her great-grandmother Jane's death twenty-five years earlier. The stone was a tempting challenge, high for such a small child, its angle not easy for climbing. But that was no detriment to an active four year old. She reached up to the top edge, fought for a footing, slipped, and then clung on once again. She had to keep climbing. And climbing. She couldn't give up because she needed to get up high, to the lip of the stone, perhaps even beyond. She needed to leave the ground with its grouping of celebrants and join the kites that beckoned high up in the bright sky.

At least that's what I thought as I watched the child's efforts. But I do not know. We were still standing respectfully around the grave. As one does of course.

BODIES IN MOTION

"Here in this island we arrived"

THE TEMPEST, I, 2

In *Biography of an Island*, Perry Westbrook tells us that after the wreck of a Nova Scotia schooner, the local fishermen of Swans Island, Maine, carried the frozen bodies of three crew members to the island cemetery and buried them there. "After a severe storm, one hesitates to probe deeply into the debris along the beaches," Westbrook wryly observes.

A body afloat is claimed by land people, escaping the control of the ever-moving sea. Culture, as represented by the land, trumps nature.

Bodies floating at large are also the concern of the United States Environmental Protection Agency. The regulations for the sea burial of "non-cremated remains" are specific: the burial must take place "at least 3 nautical miles from land and in water at least 600 feet deep." In certain areas, including parts of Florida and the Mississippi River Delta, the water must be at least 1800 feet deep. In all cases, "all necessary measure shall be taken to ensure that the remains sink to the bottom rapidly and permanently." "Full fathom five thy father lies," says Ariel to the son of the supposedly drowned king in Shakespeare's *Tempest*. For the EPA, it is important that the body be put to rest deeper than five fathoms (a fathom is six feet) and in such a way that it will not move.

The power of the sea to transform the body is not the interest of the EPA, whose concern is not only that the body stays in one spot but that any "sea-change"–as celebrated by Shakespeare's Ariel–occurs in a particularly marked place in the sea. A report of such burial must include, in addition to data on distance from shore and depth of water, the latitude and longitude of the burial location. Rules serve bureaucratic purposes, imposing order on the sea. In this case too, their very existence affirms that the intentional burials of "non-cremated" remains, though rare, do take place: a firm in Massachusetts advertises full body sea burials, and for $1750 will sell the client a special "Atlantic shroud," a kind of long bag-like anorak that comes equipped with weights. Far more usual is the burial of cremated ashes. In San Francisco alone, some twenty businesses advertise services enabling surviving family and friends of the dead to bury ashes at sea (some offering a sumptuous repast to the celebrants on board).

Physical challenges (and high cost) aside, it is clear that for most bereaved individuals, ashes in the sea are one thing, a body quite another. The body transformed to ash has already joined another–we could say, natural–element. But an intact body retains a stronger connection to us, its transformation in the sea fraught with horror and dread.

As scripted by the master playmaker Prospero, Shakespeare's shipwrecked characters have the good–or possibly, bad–fortune to arrive on the shores of a magic island where a body supposedly lying "full fathom five" can turn out not to be drowned after all. A small island off the coast of New England, site of a community economically dependent on the sea, is a different matter. Storms and other unexpected incidents at sea meant real mortality for real world islanders.

To deal with their dead, an island community sought, whenever possible, to create or impose a land-based order, to keep the dead as their own. The Gotts Islanders established a cemetery early on in their history, probably at the beginning of the nineteenth century. One can read its fixed order, the rows and markers, the wood fence, as marking the stark contrast between the finality and fixed form of the gravesite and the sea whose form is motion itself. But the islanders did not turn their backs on the sea where so many of their number would have died. To the contrary, their cemetery, like those of so many island and coastal communities, is sited almost literally on the boundary between earth and ocean. It occupies, to this degree, a margin, an in-between place where two elements intersect.

In 1896, at the height of quarrying activity on nearby Black Island, the Gotts Islanders found on their shores the bodies of two men who had drowned when their barge carrying granite to the mainland went down. Performing an office known to so many island peoples–I think again of the Swans Island account–the islanders buried these unknown bodies in their community cemetery. There were no formal grave markers, no discussions of coffins or funeral services. The community simply did what was for them the decent thing. These quarry workers were unknown men who came even from foreign countries to labor in remote places in Maine. "Italian," a notice in the Bar Harbor Herald said. No names. No one knew what parents, wives, lovers, or children awaited a return that would never come about. These men had joined in the Gotts Island cemetery an order foreign to them; they had come to a place they would never have thought of as theirs, a place that would be for them forever marginal.

The definition of order in this story, as in so many stories, is thus compromised. The logic of the land, of culture, is neither infallible nor completely distinct from that of the much less known sea. In this case the land receives what the sea has once claimed. The transformative work has ostensibly been done. But perhaps not. The very anonymity of the quarrymen consigns them to another element; ambiguity enables the imagining that belongs to the unknown. A small island cemetery is hardly to be compared to the magic island Shakespeare gives us in *The Tempest*. But here too is a site of transformation.

FENCING

It's been a hard job, he says, especially on a hot July day. John was working with three neighbors to remove all the posts and ornamental crosspieces in the cemetery fence. Each rotted and vertical post had to be pried out of its wood box-like covering and the new post pushed in to replace it. The horizontal pieces that had once graced the fence, also victims of too many Maine winters, had already been removed. And since ornamental railings are too difficult to maintain, they are to be replaced by straight horizontals. In the meantime, the old boards that once traced an intricate design lie in a pile on the ground, chipped and bleaching in the summer sun. Their work is done.

This leaves forty-two vertical posts standing alone. Two sets of much taller uprights, both facing the sun when it rises over the spruces on the top of the hill, mark the spaces where ornamental gates once opened to receive a coffin-laden wagon and thereby connect the worlds of the dead and the living.

The cemetery is a space that, in Heidegger's terms, "has been made room for," its old fence a boundary that creates a particular "presencing." With its fence in place, the island cemetery has a form that sets it apart from both the surrounding field and the nearby sea and shifting tides. But a cemetery with its fence removed is a different thing, its effect disorienting and startling. I saw the difference on a brilliantly clear early July evening when the surrounding fields glowed stunningly pink-gold, and the angle of the setting sun turned the unfenced and standing grave stones into anonymous tall dark presences. Each stone now exerted individuality not evident when the fence created a single encompassing entity. The fence told us what is a cemetery and what is a collection of unique stone grave markers that just happened to be there.

Without the fence, the community of the dead lost its coherence. The stones were, in some way, among us in a way they were not before, and as evening came on they took on a slightly eerie quality. Too close perhaps. It's not a matter of our needing a wall to mark off what the anthropologists tell us has been viewed as the "pollution" of the dead. No, that theory doesn't really work on an island where we're all thoroughly accustomed to living with the inhabitants of the cemetery and many of us will be interred there ourselves. Rather, when village of the dead loses its form, the community of the living is also diminished. The fence reinforces form and the order that make connection possible. Fixity and motion are always in play.

Established in the early nineteenth century and providing a vista that is both temporal and spatial, our small island cemetery is an enabling place. Borrowing from Michel Foucault, Elizabeth Hallam and Jenny Hockey call such a place (in *Death, Memory and Material Culture*) a "heterotopia," a site of layered meanings that bespeak our connections with a remembered past. Standing by my own son's gravesite in the fenced cemetery, I am an archaeologist of my own loss; I excavate layers of meaning: shards of the physical landscape, but also the stories, histories, myths, even fragmented objects, all markers in both personal and social memory. As the site of memory, the cemetery is a place where something happens, where memorial permanence and mutability co-exist.

Metaphors of memory, Frances Yates told us in *The Art of Memory*, are usually spatial. Akin to other animals, we humans need our physical environments, but we relate to that physical world, and we know it, in ways that depend in turn upon what we bring to it on any given occasion. Geographer Yi-Fu Tuan, in a book titled *Escapism*, writes that "Humans not only submit and adapt to 'nature,' or 'reality'; [they can] 'see' what is not there." We must then consider who we are as human "in productive tandem with the real and imagined." We draw on sites, spaces, and the relationships among them to create our own "poem" or prose narrative.

Memory, as process, is a central element in the story. Like the rocky substrate of the small Atlantic island that encodes a history of movement over eons of time, the "heterotopic" layers of place offer, in their very malleability, consolation not only for all that we do not know, cannot explain about loss and absence, but also for the very experience of not knowing. In movement and motion, however gradual, lies transformational energy. I think this is what Robert Louis Stevenson meant when he wrote more than a century ago that a writer must "know his countryside, whether real or imaginary, like his hand." Imagination and geography are two sides of the same coin. Stevenson links knowledge of what is not necessarily physically there (the "imaginary") to the physical reality of his own hand, his own physical body.

Writer Barbara Hurd movingly evokes the power of the not-there, and the capacity of the perceiving eye to fill in apparently empty spaces, when she observes the "world between grains of sand" on a beach. The spaces between the grains of sand, she says, "shift and reconfigure but never disappear." They are "*interstitial*, from the Latin root meaning to *stand between.*" New patterns, consisting of both physical elements and spaces "in between" emerge; in this continuing mobility, emptiness in transformed into occupancy.

My footsteps on the rugged granite rock slabs that ring much of the island leave, unlike Hurd's on a sandy beach, no apparent trace. Precious little sand is in sight in my island environment. Stone, literally the bedrock of my heterotopia, is an essential layer and central building block in my narrative of loss. But stone is still malleable, forms patterns, in its own way. Late eighteenth-century Maine islanders used smooth round rocks called popplestones to ballast the holds of homemade sailing vessels; later such stones were used to pave the streets of growing cities in the American Northeast. The change in function, like a re-organization of parts, is integral to the meaning and significance of the stone. Carrying within them a history, each a fragment of pre-history in fact, the stones figure metaphorically for the written pieces that together form, for me, a new story, a new landscape.

So I am fortunate that I have a "countryside." I know its rocky edges and its meandering pathways through dark and mossy woods. But the process of such knowing is continuous and never ending. Where the trail actually takes me is less important that what it invokes, what it means, along the way. In this process, the absent asserts a special presence, a necessary element in the constructive, and transformational, work that memory plays in the narrative of a life.

Yesterday, again under hot sun, a work crew of neighbors finished replacing the horizontal bars of the fence. The new streamlined version, minus the ornamental arrangement, is simple yet nonetheless satisfying. But this is Maine. And this morning, only the barest outline of the fence is visible in fog that sweeps in from the sea and circles round in its takeover over of the land. I watch two figures, neighbors whom I easily recognized as they passed close by my front door minutes ago, turn into amorphous ghosts as they enter the cemetery to visit a family gravesite. In the moving mist the line between the communities of the living and the dead is briefly elided. The white wood fence is as porous as the island's granite edges that shift with the ever-moving sea.

About the Author

Christina Marsden Gillis's work has been published in such diverse publications as *House Beautiful, Death Studies, Journal of Medical Humanities, Raritan, Island Journal, Hotel Amerika, Bellevue Literary Review,* and *Southwest Review.* Immersing herself in a specific place and teasing out the region's history, lore, and ecology, she considers herself an environmental writer who focuses on the spirit of a place, its human and natural interconnections.

In a series of powerful essays In *Where Edges Don't Hold*, Gillis shares with readers insights derived from spending every summer of her adult life on Gotts Island, off the coast of Maine.

Gillis received her doctorate in English with an emphasis in eighteenth-century literature and was the founding associate director of the Townsend Center for the Humanities at UC Berkeley. Her previous book, *Writing on Stone*, explores her special relationship with Gotts Island following the death of her son in a tragic accident.

CPSIA information can be obtained
at www.ICGtesting.com
Printed in the USA
BVHW091540090522
636559BV00011B/931